CAVE

The Earth series traces the historical significance and cultural history of natural phenomena. Written by experts who are passionate about their subject, titles in the series bring together science, art, literature, mythology, religion and popular culture, exploring and explaining the planet we inhabit in new and exciting ways.

Series editor: Daniel Allen

In the same series
Air Peter Adey
Cave Ralph Crane and Lisa Fletcher
Desert Roslynn D. Haynes
Earthquake Andrew Robinson
Fire Stephen J. Pyne
Flood John Withington
Islands Stephen A. Royle
Moon Edgar Williams
Tsunami Richard Hamblyn
Volcano James Hamilton
Water Veronica Strang
Waterfall Brian J. Hudson

Cave

Ralph Crane and Lisa Fletcher

REAKTION BOOKS

For Joy Crane and Vasil Stojcevski

Published by
Reaktion Books Ltd
33 Great Sutton Street
London EC1V ODX, UK
www.reaktionbooks.co.uk

First published 2015

Printed and bound in China by 1010 Printing International Ltd

A catalogue record for this book is available from the British Library

ISBN 978 1 78023 431 1

CONTENTS

Preface

'It's not what you'd expect, down there,' he had said.
'It's not like above-ground folks would expect.'
Robert Penn Warren, *The Cave* (1959)

Caves are fundamental to human history. They are simultaneously places of shelter and places of deep, dark danger. They are places of birth and of burial, dwelling places and sanctuaries from persecution. They are a human habitat and the home of mythical monsters.

For many people, a cave is simply a natural underground chamber which has been formed over hundreds of thousands of years; however, as Chapter One demonstrates, the term 'cave' is far from straightforward. In addressing the question of what is and what is not a cave, that chapter sets the parameters for the rest of the book, and highlights the anthropocentric ways we talk about caves. The next two chapters provide an introduction to the science of caves, how caves – and the speleothems such as stalactites and stalagmites which decorate them – are formed, how plants and animals living in the various zones of caves have adapted to their hostile habitat, and how humans have used caves over the millennia. The remaining six chapters focus on human interactions with caves, both literal and metaphorical. Caves pose questions about the relationships between humans and the way they imagine and attempt to define their natural environment. They are places that at once evoke fear and loathing, and awe and inspiration. First investigated by humans

Wes Skiles, *Lure of the Labyrinth*, Ginnie Springs, Florida.

7

as sites of shelter, caves have long been explored for pleasure and, like mountains and other natural landforms and landscapes, they have attracted adventurers who are lured by the challenge of overcoming danger, and driven by the desire to go where no human being has gone before. They have also attracted writers, artists and photographers who have shown us new and varied ways to see and think about caves. And most of the world's major religions venerate caves associated with a divinity or a holy person who may have taken shelter there. Our continuing fascination with caves is evident in the fact that each year more than twenty million people visit tourist caves in almost 100 countries, with Mammoth Cave in Kentucky alone attracting over two million visitors annually.

Our book celebrates caves as wonders of nature and as habitats for flora and fauna, but above all it emphasizes the roles caves have played and continue to play in the human experience.

1 What is a Cave?

The *Oxford English Dictionary* defines 'cave' as 'a hollow place opening more or less horizontally under the ground; a cavern, den, habitation in the earth'. This seemingly simple word, derived via French from the Latin *cavum* meaning 'hollow', has no exact synonyms in English. There are associated words in etymological terms ('cavern', 'cavity') and semantically ('grotto', 'abyss', 'den'), but 'cave' carries a heavy load. C.H.D. Cullingford, the editor of the 1953 speleological classic *British Caving*, apologizes for 'the overworked "cave"',[1] but explains that repetition is unavoidable – he allows 'cavern', for instance, only 'in the more limited sense of a chamber within a cave system'. Despite the apparent singularity of the word 'cave', there is ultimately no straightforward answer to the question, 'What is a cave?' A standard scientific response defines a cave as 'a natural void beneath the land surface that is large enough to admit humans'.[2] Isolated subterranean cavities, or 'vugs', with no opening to the surface are not caves, although they may eventually become caves if the movement of water, or the breakdown of rock, links them to the surface and thus they are sometimes termed 'entranceless caves'. Voids hollowed out of the earth by humans (mines, drains, tunnels, shelters or dwellings) are not caves, but they may connect to caves, or permit access to once entranceless caves. An opening or recess in the earth which cannot be described as a 'void' – a rock shelter or cliff-side overhang – is not a cave, but if its darker pockets contain mineral formations typical of a 'true cave', or provide habitat for organisms which

populate caves, it may be described as a 'borderline cave'. Perhaps most importantly, a hole or fissure in rock too small to admit a human body is not a cave; in caver parlance it does not 'go', but for scientists it may turn out to be a 'protocave' if hydrological or geological processes widen the cave to allow human entry. Caves, in short, are always defined and depicted in relation to humans.

Not only do scientists measure and define hollows under the earth in relation to the dimensions of the human body, but the scientific and non-scientific literature of caves is a powerful reminder of our inability to comprehend natural phenomena except in relation to ourselves. In her poem 'Earth, Air, Water, Fire: A Love Poem in Four Elements', Tasmanian poet Adrienne Eberhard writes 'We carry caves inside us: / the heart's dark chambers, / water-washed cavern of the womb, / limestone pockets of the brain'.[3] The fundamental dualisms of surface/depth and light/dark, which delineate actual caves for scientists, are also crucial to the symbolic roles caves have played in the human imagination throughout history. In both scientific and non-scientific language, the lexicon of cave description is fundamentally dependent on the vocabulary of human life on the surface. In fact and fiction, the features of caves are frequently named after parts of the human body and, more

Features of a typical limestone cave:
1 stalactite
2 stalagmite
3 column
4 chimney
5 traverse
6 sump
7 duck
8 aven
9 impermeable rock capping
10 stream sink or swallet
11 resurgence
12 fault
13 streamway
14 limestone escarpment
15 grotto
16 breakdown chamber
17 blind pit

extensively, the spaces and structures of human buildings. Cave openings are gaping 'mouths' into the dark 'gullets' of the earth, or ruptures in the planet's 'skin' which lead to the 'bowels' of the earth. Just as often, in countless diverse texts, the depths of caves are depicted by comparison to human biology: 'As if this hollow in the earth lived and thought and breathed in its own way, throbbing with the slow pulse of water.'[4] The ubiquity of architectural metaphors in descriptions of caves is especially striking and suggests an overwhelming tendency to see caves as analogues for human phenomena: caves are 'chambers', 'vaults' or 'cathedrals'; they have 'doorways', 'floors', 'walls', 'ceilings', 'rooms', 'domes' and 'chimneys'. The richly metaphoric vocabulary of caves exposes the inadequacy of words to accurately and fully describe the deep, dark places of the earth. While the impossibility of capturing the earth's reality in words is not peculiar to the spaces beneath its surface, cave literature frequently reveals a heightened awareness of the limits of language in relation to natural phenomena.

Not only are caves off the map of everyday life, the dark depths of caves – especially water-filled caves – extend well

Entrance to
Sassafras Cave,
Tasmania, Australia.

beyond the reach of even the most determined explorers. As the first four chapters of this book explain, the development of a specialized discourse about caves, with its own finely calibrated descriptive and analytical vocabulary and a coherent body of literature, is remarkably recent. While studies of caves had been published as early as the sixteenth century, a genuine and co-ordinated discipline into the exploration of caves did not emerge until the last decades of the nineteenth century. Both the actual *and* imagined journeys into caves are inescapably experienced from the perspective of human life on the surface and in the light.

Whereas the standard, scientific definition of a cave uses the human body as a yardstick for subterranean spaces, non-scientific genres and subjects such as literature, film, mythology and art use caves as conceptual tools to measure and evaluate the human condition. This book discusses the history of ideas about caves across diverse areas of human endeavour; it examines the representation of caves throughout history by scholars, scientists and explorers who seek to understand them as natural phenomena. It also considers the multifarious cultural roles caves have played and continue to play – as sources for artistic and literary inspiration, as sacred sites and places for worship, as symbols and settings in folklore and mythology, and as spectacles for leisure and tourism. The goal throughout is to reflect on the diversity of ways, both material and symbolic, in which caves have been exploited for human use.

David Gillieson, an expert in the conservation and management of caves and karst, suggests that the rule of human entry implies a minimum cave diameter of 0.3 m, while one character in Robert Penn Warren's novel *The Cave* (1959) jokes that 'a cave is no place for a fat man.'[5] For cavers, a passage which tests these dimensions is a 'squeeze' or a 'restriction' but, as there is no relationship between the size of an entrance and the size of the cave beyond, explorers will push themselves into any potential opening, no matter how tight the fit. For author and expeditioner Michael Ray Taylor a squeeze is 'any crawlway whose passage requires the removal of gear, clothing or skin'.[6] The importance of the human body to the threshold between impassable hole or crack and 'true cave' is clear in some of the more comic names for tight passages in American caves, such as 'Fat Man's Misery' in Mammoth Cave, Kentucky, the 'Gun Barrel' in Knox Cave, New York, the 'Worm Squirm' in California Caverns and 'Crisco Crack' in Great Expectations (or 'Great X') Cave, in Wyoming. Great X is also notorious for a 300-m tube known as the 'Grim Crawl of Death'. Taylor describes the panic of being caught by the 'Devil's Pinch' in the Bone-Norman system, West Virginia:

> I felt panic rising and paused to breathe deeply – but I was in too far. As I inhaled, my ribs swelled against the constriction and stopped. I could take only half breaths, could move forward only when I exhaled. What if I exhaled too much? What if I reached a point where I couldn't inhale at all?[7]

The question of human entry is central to cave science and exploration – to those who strive to discover new routes beneath the earth or 'virgin passages'. But for non-cavers, the idea of going underground stimulates horror as often as it inspires exploration and adventure, not least because of the powerful association of caves with tombs. In 2005 three horror films depicted cave explorers trapped underground and hunted by monstrous predators. *The Cavern* was promoted with the tagline 'Some places should never be explored', and posters for *The Cave* declared, 'There are places man was never meant to go.' The publicity for the splatter-fest *The Descent* invited filmgoers to 'Face your deepest fear' and was explicit about the psychological risks of venturing underground: 'When you're trapped 2 miles underground there are many ways to lose your mind . . . Claustrophobia. Disorientation. Isolation. Paranoia. Terror.'

Thinking about caves inevitably means thinking about how humans fit within them and, certainly in the popular imagination, caves stir primal fears of being buried alive, or trapped in the dark with mysterious or malevolent forces

Cover design for the single magazine edition (#1 of 5) of Jeff Parker and Steve Lieber's *Underground* (2009).

much more often than they arouse positive emotions. When Clarice Starling ventures into the stony labyrinth beneath the serial killer's house in Jonathan Demme's *The Silence of the Lambs*, she descends into a metaphoric 'cave'. Viewers watch Clarice – trembling and terrified – through the killer's night-vision goggles as she stumbles blindly along the humid, utterly dark passages of Buffalo Bill's basement. The visual

Théodore Caruelle
d'Aligny, *Landscape
with a Cave*, c. 1830s,
oil on canvas.

imagery of a cave-like space heightens our emotional iden-
tification with Clarice, and symbolizes the dark recesses of the
mind of the madman who hunts her. The shock of this scene,
of course, is that we share Bill's point of view and thus are
provoked to contemplate the darkness within ourselves. Such
employment of cave imagery to cue emotional and intellectual responses is one aspect of the 'complex negotiations of
nature and culture',[8] which reveals that the long history of
human engagement with the natural world has shaped our
view of ourselves.

For centuries, caves have been routinely employed in Western philosophy and literature to symbolize the dark spots in the human psyche, both for the individual and collectively. Thinkers from Plato to Freud use caves as analogues for regimes of ignorance and unreality, as containers for buried secrets and forgotten dreams, and to signify the polar opposite of whole sight or true knowledge. In *The Republic* Plato uses the Allegory of the Cave (also known as the Simile of the Cave, the Analogy of the Cave and Plato's Cave) to dramatize the philosopher's ascent from darkness to light, from unreality to reason. Plato asks us to 'Imagine an underground chamber like a cave, with a long entrance open to the daylight and as wide as the cave' in which men have been imprisoned their entire lives, chained with their backs to the entrance so that they can only see the cave wall before them.[9] A large fire burns behind the prisoners and a procession of men carrying stone figures passes above them, casting shadows as in a puppet show onto the cave wall. The prisoners, who know nothing beyond the cave, perceive the shadows to be the 'whole truth'.[10] Plato depicts the painful experience of a prisoner released from his 'delusions', 'forcibly dragged up the steep and rugged ascent and not let go till he had been dragged out into the sunlight'.[11] Over time, the prisoner embraces his liberation as he connects 'the ascent into the upper world and the sight of the objects there with the upward progress of the mind into the intelligible region'; but his education is not complete until he accepts his responsibility to return to the cave, to live once again with the unenlightened and 'get used to seeing in the dark'.[12]

The powerful association of light with knowledge (and darkness with ignorance) also underpins the use of cave metaphors in theories of dreams and the unconscious, most famously by Sigmund Freud and Carl Jung. In *The Interpretation of Dreams*, Freud implicitly includes caves in the suite of dream images representing the female body, with 'cavities, ships, and all kinds of vessels'.[13] In 1909, while travelling with Freud in America, Jung dreamed of discovering a cave beneath the cellar of his house. In his memoirs, written over twenty years later,

'Grotto of Adelsberg –
Carinthia', illustration
from *Famous Caverns
and Grottoes*, by W. H.
Davenport Adams
(1886).

he gives more detail about the dream and describes a 'choked-up
cave' with multiple levels – 'Neolithic tools' on the dusty floor
of the upper levels and remnants of prehistoric fauna below.
Jung interpreted his dreamed journey through the house
into the cave below as a symbolic passage through 'past times
and passed stages of consciousness', but in relation to the

A cave map of
Witches Cave II with
Shuttleworth Pot
Entrance, Cumbria.

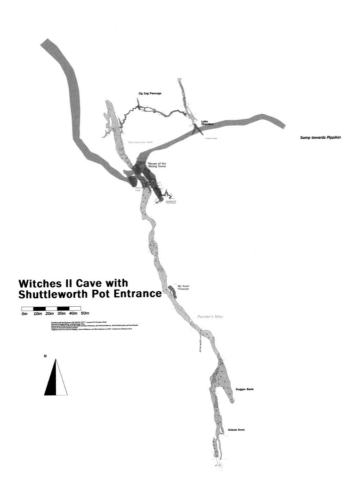

**Witches II Cave with
Shuttleworth Pot Entrance**

0m   10m   20m   30m   40m   50m

N

individual's foundations in cultural memory. Jung continued writing of the dream for nearly 30 years because it was his 'first inkling of a collective *a priori* beneath the personal psyche'.[14] Going into caves represents, for Plato, Freud and Jung, a return to some prior state of existence; caves are thus claimed as settings for key stages in an overarching human story, rather than of interest or value *as* caves.

The classification of caves as openings in the earth accessible to humans is symptomatic of a powerful anthropocentric bias in the history of ideas about the earth. Caves, while we can only apprehend their reality through the matrices of language and culture, undeniably have a literal and physical truth that exceeds our grasp. They are, after all, formed in rock over millennia. Perhaps more importantly, caves (in themselves and as fragments of larger natural systems) have meaning and value 'independent of the usefulness of the non-human world for human purposes'.[15] Gillieson offers a 'strictly scientific definition' which includes no mention of humans: *A cave is a natural cavity in a rock which acts as a conduit for water flow between input points, such as streamsinks, and output points, such as springs or seeps.*[16] Is there a way to think about caves in which humans are not dominant, or is our knowledge of natural phenomena so inflected by culture that we are fundamentally unable to remove ourselves from any picture or story of caves? Would a geocentric approach to caves be just as limiting as foregrounding human interaction with caves? After all, it is fundamentally inaccurate to omit humans from the natural world, or to assume that 'nature is only authentic if we are entirely absent from it.'[17] In historical and cultural terms, caves are always much more than functions of geological and hydrological processes. The question 'What is a cave?' has no easy or conclusive answer because of the countless ways in which caves signify and function in relation to people, and because of the myriad ways in which caves interact with non-human organisms.

The entrance to a cave is not a clearly defined doorway between the environment above ground and the one below, but a zone of transition. To enter a cave is to move towards utter darkness. The journey begins at the entrance – striding on foot beneath a colossal archway, crawling on hands and knees through a tangle of vines and spiderwebs, or wriggling flat on one's belly into a muddy hole. Cave surveyors often locate the boundary between inside and outside at the 'drip line', beyond which rain does not fall to the ground. The entrance zone – which varies from a narrow and exposed space of less than a metre for a small crevice on barren ground, to several hundred metres of thriving ecosystem for a large, open entrance in a forested valley – is the furthest most people will ever venture into 'wild caves'. In tourist caves or 'show caves', artificial light and paved pathways conceal the subtle transition between the entrance zone and the darker zone where sunlight still penetrates. This 'twilight zone' is darker and more humid than the surface and the insulation of rock walls and reduced airflow makes for a more stable temperature, but enough daylight penetrates to sustain some plant life and to orient the human visitor. Barbara Hurd describes the view from this 'place of the in-between' in Devil's Hole, Maryland:

> From where I'm standing, I can look down and to the right,
> farther into the cave, and see how the black gets denser,
> takes on substance, fills in every crack. Or I can look up,
> to the left, and still see, not sky, but at least the brown rocks
> and obvious handholds, small protrusions, even an insect
> in the air.[18]

The truly dark zone, in which only organisms adapted to a complete and perpetual darkness can dwell full-time, maintains a near-constant temperature close to the mean annual temperature on the surface. It may extend for hundreds of kilometres and take the explorer thousands of metres beneath the surface. The longest surveyed cave system, Mammoth Cave in Kentucky, extends over 620 km – well ahead of the second longest, Jewel Cave in South Dakota (over 260 km). The two deepest known caves are in Europe: Krubera (or Voronya) Cave (2,191 m) and Illyuzia-Mezhonnogo-Snezhnaya (1,753 m), both in Abkhazia, Georgia.

The atmospheric stability of inner caves and the near absence of organic matter mean that to enter a cave is to change it – however lightly one treads. Human bodies move the air and increase the temperature; clothes shed lint which sticks to moist walls and formations; feet and hands leave impressions on floors and walls; and skin cells, hair and perspiration raise the levels of organic matter in an environment which may have been virtually unchanged for centuries. In the late 1970s, a team of cavers

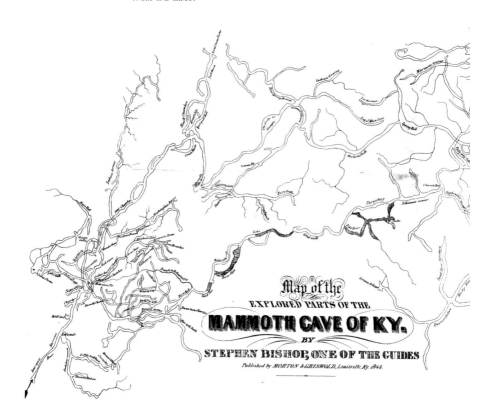

'Map of the Explored Parts of the Mammoth Cave of KY', Kentucky, by Stephen Bishop.

surveying Jaguar Cave in Tennessee found human footprints in a remote passage; archaeologists later identified 274 distinct footprints left by nine individuals and used radiocarbon-dating of torch charcoal residue to conclude that these 'prehistoric cavers' had ventured into the truly dark zone of Jaguar Cave 5,400 years earlier.[19] Passionate cavers thus fight an internal battle between their deep desire to get underground and their commitment to preserving the pristine, often fragile beauty of environments formed over millennia.

In the dark depths of caves humidity is constantly high, and the atmosphere can be near saturated with water vapour; perhaps this explains why literary characters in caves often ask, 'Can you breathe darkness instead of air?'[20] The heroine of Nevada Barr's caving thriller *Blind Descent* (2009) experiences the 'shock of light deprivation' deep in Lechuguilla Cave, New

Mexico: 'It was not a mere absence of light, it was a substance, an element, a suffocating miasma that filled her ears, clogged her nostrils, bore down on her shoulders and chest.'[21] In some caves the air *is* dangerous due to high concentrations of carbon dioxide, a colourless, odourless gas which tastes slightly acidic (although not to everyone). Breathing air with a concentration of carbon dioxide greater than 0.5 per cent – or 'foul air' – even briefly, rapidly increases heart and breathing rates and prolonged exposure leads to unconsciousness, suffocation and death. 'Foul air' (the term itself is further evidence of anthropocentrism) can be both a natural phenomenon and the consequence of human activity on the surface. For instance, the Bungonia Caves in New South Wales, Australia, have unusually high levels of foul air due to the decomposition of masses of organic matter washed into the cave during heavy rainfall and a lack of ventilation. The carbon dioxide-rich air in Kacna jama, Slovenia, is caused by the seepage underground of waste from a paper mill – a reminder that even the remotest cave passages are parts of integrated natural systems which link the earth's surface and its depths.

There are no clear divisions between the three cave 'zones' – or indeed between the cave and the surface environment – especially in meteorological and ecological terms. The transition from one zone to the next is gradual and the constant flow of air, water, sediment, animals and organic matter through the cave means that they are better understood as integrated spaces. In Sherod Santos's poem 'Fermanagh Cave' (1999), a boy and his father stumble on a cave by following a stream and inch their way underground 'step by step along the wet-ribbed walls'; in the cave's 'deeper reaches' they can hear 'the slub / of water riddling through the muck'.[22] The most important element linking the earth's surface and its hollow depths is water. Water percolates underground through soil and porous rock, trickles through fissures in bedrock, or rushes in a tumbling torrent along subterranean streams or rivers. Thinking about caves should also involve thinking about the distinctiveness of the surface landscape – the 'sinks' and 'swells' above the 'folded hollow darkness'.[23]

Cave wall, main chamber, Gaping Ghyll, Yorkshire.

The term 'karst' denotes a landscape dominated by features formed mainly through the dissolution of bedrock: closed depressions (sinkholes in the u.s. and dolines in Europe), subterranean drainage systems and caves. Approximately 15 per cent of the planet's surface is karst and around 25 per cent of the world's population depends on karst groundwater for survival.[24] Karstic terrain is principally formed in limestone – a sedimentary rock comprised mainly of calcium carbonate – but solution caves also occur in other carbonates, mainly dolomite, in evaporates such as gypsum and halite and, less commonly, in other forms of rock including sandstone and basalt. Cave scientists distinguish between the geomorphology of 'true karst' – formed principally through the solution of rock by water – and 'pseudokarst' – in which caves and associated landforms develop through processes other than solution, from the weathering of rock by wind and rain or the erosive effects of turbulent melt water, to the flow of lava or the fracturing of rock by tectonic movements. However caves are formed, they are best conceived as fragments of larger systems in both space and time; simply, a cave is always part of a whole.

Cave Coral, Orient
Cave, Jenolan Caves,
New South Wales,
Australia.

2 Speaking of Speleology

Speleology is the scientific study of caves. On 4 August 1893, speaking at a meeting of the Association Française pour l'Avancement des Sciences, the French lawyer and cave explorer E. A. Martel used this 'not very graceful word' to name a field of study which he argued 'claims a place among the sciences'.[1] Martel credited the prehistorian Emile Rivière with creating the term in around 1890 from the Greek σπήλαιον (cave) and λόγος (discourse), but Martel's is the first published definition and discussion of the term. Speleology is not, however, the earliest word used to denote the study of caves. In 1850 Adolf Schmidl, celebrated by Martel as 'the real originator of speleology or the scientific study of caves',[2] proposed the term *Höhlenkunde*, literally 'cave study', during a talk to a learned society in Vienna. *Höhlenkunde* has endured in German, as has the related term *Höhlenforschung* (cave exploration), alongside the more technical term *Speläologie*. Other efforts to coin a moniker under which cave scientists could work together were less successful. W. S. Forwood, in his 1870 study of Mammoth Cave, offered 'caveology', and in 1889 Martel experimented fleetingly with a pair of terms – *grottologie* for the study and exploration of caves and *grottisme* for the sport of caving – before settling on the term we use today. Thanks to Martel, since the mid-1890s, scientists have been speaking of 'speleology'.

Scientists and explorers had, in fact, been studying caves for centuries before the term 'speleology' was coined, but their activities had been mostly disjointed and uncoordinated. A long tradition of cave exploration and scholarship did exist in Slovenia where, since the seventeenth century, men who ventured underground were aware of the work of those who had preceded them. For instance, nineteenth-century explorers of Postojnska jama (the Slovenian word for cave) such as Schmidl, Franz Kraus and Martel joined a long line of adventurers, writers and scientists who had set out before them to map, sketch and describe the caves of Slovenia's limestone terrain.

The first published map of a Slovenian cave was drawn by Johann Weichard von Valvasor. He actively explored the caves of his region from 1678 to 1689 and sought to understand the behaviour of subterranean drainage systems. For the cave science historian Trevor Shaw, Baron Valvasor was the 'first true speleologist' for both the fullness of his descriptions and his original observation that caves and subterranean waterways are parts of larger hydrological systems.[3] Shaw also acknowledges the eighteenth-century Austrian court mathematician, Joseph Anton Nagel, as a 'speleologist' working well before such a classification existed. Nagel crawled underground in Austria, Slovenia and Moravia (now in the Czech Republic) on the orders of Emperor Franz I and produced long illustrated reports of his observations. In Slovenia, Nagel drew remarkably accurate plans of uncharted caves including Postojnska jama and Socerbska jama, travelled 660 m underground in Planinska jama and reached the underground river Pivka through Črna jama. The historical significance of Slovenia for the scientific study of caves inheres in the term karst, which derives from the name of the high barren limestone region south of Ljubljana – the Kras Plateau. Karst is the root word in a whole suite of specialist terms in cave hydrology and geology, from pseudokarst for landscapes analogous to karst but formed by non-dissolutional processes, to epikarst for the highly porous uppermost zone of soluble rock, and paleokarst for ancient karst features dating from an earlier period of karstification. 'Karst' entered the English language as a term to classify limestone topography in 1894, when it began to be used in the journal of the Royal Geographical Society. In the final years of the nineteenth century

and into the first decades of the twentieth, the scientific study of caves rapidly grew into a legitimate academic field of international significance – in large degree due to the efforts of Martel. However, the discourse of speleology has never been strictly scientific; from Martel's time to the present day, it has embraced adventure alongside scientific investigation, both of which have characterized journeys into caves for centuries.

Plate from William Buckland, *Reliquiae Diluvianae* (1823).

William Buckland, who wrote the first great classic of British speleology, *Reliquiae Diluvianae; Or, Observations on the Organic Remains Contained in Caves, Fissures, and Diluvial Gravel, and on Other Geological Phenomena, Attesting the Action of an Universal Deluge* (1823), would have had no sense of himself as a member of a community of *cave* explorers or scientists, nor would he have thought of his research first and foremost in relation to a tradition of cave scholarship. Instead Buckland, in the book's dedication to Shute Barrington, Lord Bishop of

Durrington, thanks his Lordship for indulging Buckland's endeavours to cultivate the 'new and interesting science' of geology. *Reliquiae Diluvianae* is a report on his excavations in 1821 of Kirkdale Cavern, Yorkshire, for which he was awarded the Royal Society's Copley medal. For a contemporary reader, the drama and interest of this book comes from the tension between Buckland's passionate allegiance to geology and his religious faith. Three years earlier Buckland had used his inaugural lecture as Reader in Geology at the University of Oxford to reassure his audience that geology posed no threat to the Bible's account of the planet's history. The floors of caves contained evidence, he argued, for the 'universal deluge' or Noah's flood (though he abandoned this idea in the 1830s). In 1823 Buckland became the first person to discover fossil human remains when he unearthed a human skeleton covered in red ochre in Paviland or Goat's Hole Cave in South Wales but, partly because of his Old Testament view of human history, he did not recognize that the remains were prehistoric and thus did not appreciate the full significance of his discovery. By 1874, when the second book in the British speleological canon, William Boyd Dawkins's *Cave Hunting: Researches on the Evidence of Caves Respecting the Early Inhabitants of Europe*, was published, some kind of collective identity for cave scientists was beginning to form.

Dawkins describes a 'new science of cave-hunting' comprised of two integrated divisions of study – the physical (geology, physics, chemistry) and the biological (archaeology, history). His book begins by tracing the 'legends and superstitions connected with caves' throughout human history:

> It is, indeed, no wonder that legends and poetical fancies such as these should cluster round caves, for the gloom of their recesses, and the shrill drip of the water from the roof, or the roar of the subterranean water-falls echoing through the passages, and the white bosses of stalagmite looming like statues through the darkness, offer ample materials for the use of a vivid imagination.[4]

Drapery speleothems in Orient Cave, Jenolan Caves, New South Wales, Australia.

Dawkins presents the 'cave-hunter' as a figure of an advanced intellectual age in which scientists could work unhindered by pagan superstitions or religious dogma. While Buckland 'laid the foundations of the new science of cave-hunting in this country', he belonged to a 'scientific world . . . not then sufficiently educated to accept the antiquity of the human race'.[5] The first chapter of *Cave Hunting* is a plea for the potential of caves as sites and topics of serious research in established academic disciplines. Dawkins traces the history of European cave exploration to insist that by 1874 it was 'impossible to shut our eyes to the continuity that exists between geology, archæology, biology, and history – sciences which at first sight appear isolated from each other',[6] but the book's stated scholarly ambitions cannot conceal the degree to which Dawkins's excitement about working underground is a function of both his intellectual curiosity and the pull caves exert on his 'vivid imagination'. Just by introducing himself as a 'cave-hunter' – an adventurer heading into the dark and the deep to seek the secrets of the earth – Dawkins keeps in play the cluster of fanciful ideas about caves, which he otherwise dismisses as unscientific.

The fantasy of a hidden subterranean world where explorers and scientists might find clues to solve the great mysteries of our planet reached the height of its appeal in the closing decades of the nineteenth century. George Hartwig's popular science book *The Subterranean World*, first published in 1871, describes 'dark regions . . . which are sometimes beneficent and sometimes disastrous to mankind'. His depiction of a 'hidden world' of secrets and 'treasures' is redolent with the same images and metaphors as the 'lost world' adventure novels popular at the time. The knowledge and resources to be discovered in the 'subterranean world', in Hartwig's terms, aid the advancement of humanity. 'Man' turns underground to look upon its 'wonders' and to 'make its treasures subservient to his wants':[7]

> There lie concealed the mysterious laboratories of fire,
> which reveal to us their existence in earthquakes and
> volcanic explosions. There, in successive strata, repose the

remains of extinct animals and plants. There many a wonderful cavern may be seen, with its fantastic stalactites, its rushing waters, and its noble halls. There have been deposited the rich stores of mineral wealth – the metals, the coals, the salt, the sulphur, &c. – without whose aid man would never have been more than a savage.[8]

Yongcheon Cave, Jeju Island, South Korea.

Formal, coordinated networks of scientists and explorers who shared a passion for caves began to emerge in the 1880s with the establishment of cave-exploring societies across Europe. The first group, the Verein für Höhlenkunde, was founded by Franz Kraus in Vienna in 1879; their newsletter was the world's first serial devoted to the study of caves. By the end of the century, ten speleological societies were active in Europe; the most important of these for the future of serious cave research was Martel's Société de Spéléologie, established in Paris in 1895. Until the early decades of the twentieth century, geologists, archaeologists and other scientists who ventured underground did not share a specialized vocabulary with which to describe caves in rich detail, advance their theories about cave formation or classify the life forms they discovered in the damp and the dark. All in a rush, it seems, caves in Europe became hives of activity as amateur enthusiasts and professional scientists strove to discover as much as they could about underground environments and, at the same time, to develop a lexicon and theoretical base for 'speaking of speleology'. It is remarkable, for instance, how many of the specialist terms in a cave expert's glossary appeared between 1880 and 1920 – from words to describe surface karstic terrain (doline, karren) to names for solution formations (helictite, frostwork), from the master term for designating rock capable of transmitting and storing water (aquifer) to the pair of descriptors for distinguishing between minerals or sediments transported to caves from elsewhere (allogenic) and geological materials formed *in situ* (authigenic).

The term 'vadose', a 'mystic speleological password',[9] came into usage around 1894 to denote the zone in karstic terrain in which water descends through partially air-filled voids – a few years after the closely related 'phreatic', for the lower zone in which active cave passages are completely filled with water. It is perhaps no surprise that this flurry to build knowledge about the subterranean blank spaces on the world map reached its height in Britain and mainland Europe in the wake of the massive intellectual and theological shake-up provoked by Charles Darwin's theory of evolution, and at precisely the same time the major powers were scrambling for the biggest share of the planet's surface. Post-Darwin it became harder to sustain confidence in the separation of the human and animal worlds and, more broadly, in our ability to triumph over nature. At the same time, European imperialism promoted fantasies of discovery, adventure and conquest in 'primitive' landscapes. The desire to forge new frontiers became mingled with a desire to trace our evolutionary roots, as exemplified by H. Rider Haggard in his two most famous high-imperialist fictions, *King Solomon's Mines* (1885) and *She* (1886). Clearly this period was pivotal in the history of cave science, but the story of speleology's rapid growth is even today still only in its early chapters.

In 1953 C.H.D. Cullingford, an early British authority on caving, described speleology as 'an infant science'.[10] Then, only thirteen years later, T. D. Ford and Cullingford wrote in *The Science of Speleology* that the field was 'advancing at a phenomenal rate'. Their definition of speleology is inclusive: 'It is a science in which all the other scientific disciplines are in some aspect applicable to caves or their contents.'[11] In 2007 Derek Ford and Paul Williams wrote in the preface to the revised edition of their highly regarded *Karst Hydrogeology and Geomorphology* of an explosion of interest in all things cave and karst related. Nevertheless, despite the passion and commitment of an ever-growing community of dedicated cave scientists, their field has not achieved the academic status of the more traditional disciplines; this may be because with the 'proliferation of scientific material and the diversification of disciplines involved . . . it is not easy to maintain a grasp of the status of karst research'.[12] 'Caves', underground explorer and cartographer Patricia Kambesis explains, 'have not generally attracted the attention of mainstream scientists.'[13]

Speleology today, as its early founders anticipated, is a multidisciplinary field embracing the theories and practices of diverse scientific fields and subfields – including, but not limited to, geology, chemistry, hydrology, botany, biology and archaeology. Thus each speleologist looks into caves equipped with the key concepts and questions prioritized by his or her disciplinary training and specialization. Further, 'More than any other science, speleology is closely tied to exploration and adventure.'[14] The lenses through which cave scientists look underground are tinted and shaped as much by their passion for caving, and their attraction to the aesthetics and drama of karst landscapes, as they are by the theories and methodologies of hard science. The novelist Amitav Ghosh writes that 'a landscape . . . is not unlike a book – a compilation of pages that overlap without any two ever being the same', and this is as true

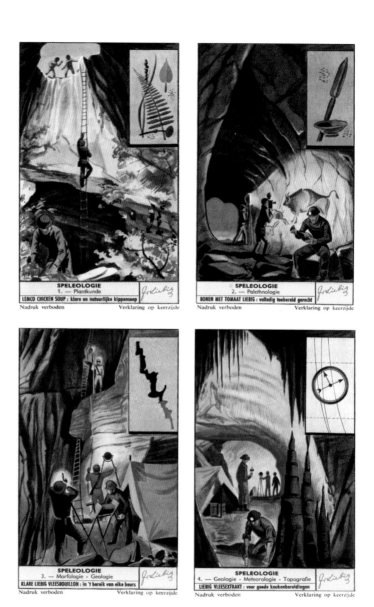

Trading cards ('Speleologie', 4 of 6) issued by the Liebig Company, Belgium, 1956.

of the depths of karst as it is of its surfaces. Ghosh explains that 'People open the book according to their taste and training, their memories and desires: for a geologist the compilation opens at one page', for a biologist another, and still another for an archaeologist, a cave cartographer and so on. 'On occasion these pages are ruled with lines that are invisible to some people, while being real for others, as real, as charged and as volatile as high-voltage cables.'[15]

Twilight Cave, Mauritius.

    The idea that caves are like books or archives is a common one in introductions to cave science. For instance, in their *Encyclopedia of Caves*, William B. White and David C. Culver write that 'Cave deposits are a history book for the ice ages.'[16] Related metaphors are used again and again throughout the literature of speleology: deep passages are 'libraries' for hydrologists and geophysicists; decorated chambers are 'galleries' for geologists and mineralogists; and cave floors are 'repositories' for geomorphologists and archaeologists. Thus, caves can be regarded as natural museums in which evidence of past climate, past geomorphic processes, past vegetation, past animals and past people will be found by those who are persistent and know how to read the pages of earth history displayed for them.[17]

The idea that caves are, or contain, texts for us to read – or that we could read if only we knew how – is a powerful one for cave scientists and explorers, who are very often the same people.

There is a basic conflict underlying all cave science between the drive to fully know and explore the subterranean environment and the recognition that one cannot ever actually *see* a cave in its entirety. Caves thus always retain a degree of mystery, even for experts who have spent their entire career studying these 'lightless labyrinths of thought'.[18] Not only do speleologists work in the dark in a quite literal sense – able only to see the segment of cave illuminated by their headlamps – but they are also continually reminded that their view of any cave, in a broader sense, is always partial and incomplete. The richest written descriptions, the most detailed maps and section diagrams, the best-lit photographs and films, and even the most advanced computer-generated simulations of caves and cave formations are always incomplete records.

After caving itself, the activity that most brings together dedicated cave explorers and cave scientists is the production of cave maps. The celebrated scientist and speleologist Arthur N. Palmer identifies cave mapping as an 'essential skill for any speleologist' and 'the first step in obtaining quantitative data about caves'.[19] Most first-generation maps are drawn on paper using data collected underground with the aid of a compass, inclinometer and tape. In the last decade, computer-based mapping techniques and geographic information and positioning systems have 'revolutionised the mapping and graphic portrayal of karst and caves'.[20]

However sophisticated cartographic methods might become, the explanation for the importance of mapping to the exploration and study of caves remains simple:

From the earliest days, cavers have prepared cave maps. The reason is simple. On the land surface, a view from a high ridge or an over flight in a small plane gives an excellent perspective of the landscape. However, one cannot see a cave. A caver can see only a small section of passage at any one time. Without mapping, cavers must depend on memory and have no way to accurately display the layout of the cave or to share their discoveries with others.[21]

Every map or model we have of a cave is a pictorial reconstruction of a place that one can only actually see and experience in fragments – and this is true whether the map is a two-dimensional sketch produced on-site with measuring tape, paper and pencil, or a three-dimensional perspective plot, generated with the aid of cutting-edge computer software. Cave explorers and speleologists have developed a series of conventions for mapping and illustrating caves, which depend, in large part, on slicing through the earth on an imagined two-dimensional plane. This conceptual and imaginative ability to 'see' through rock and earth – to picture a cave in 'plan' or 'section' – has certainly enhanced the capacity to build and communicate scientific knowledge about caves, but 'x-ray' views of subterranean environments can also perpetuate the idea that caves are discrete places with solid boundaries – walls, ceilings and floors – and clear entrances and exits.

Until the 1960s, 'all caves were thought of as ending.'[22] Cave databases listed caves that were clearly small fragments of a larger relict drainage system as distinct, separate caves. The implicit assumption that the most important measure of a cave – the factor that defined its beginning and end – was its openness to human exploration in the present also meant that every passage accessible through one entrance was catalogued as part of the same cave. A large cave might thus contain dry passages dating to the Pleistocene period *and* still-active stream passages – 'No matter, it was considered to be a single cave.'[23] The perception of caves as separate, bounded places persists in the popular imagination; in literature and film, caves

Reflections, Honeycomb Cave, Tasmania, Australia.

are often no more than underground analogues for the rooms and buildings humans inhabit on the earth's surface. But in speleological discourse, this limited view gradually gave way in the middle and later decades of the twentieth century to a more holistic view of caves as fragments of larger systems: 'individual caves' were reconceived 'as simply puzzle pieces of a larger master drainage system'.[24]

Caves are not discrete, bounded spaces; not only are they defined by their openness to the surface, but the layers of soil and rock above and around them are porous and permeable. Water seeps through carbonate rocks, trickles along narrow fissures, and gushes through larger cavities, carrying natural and man-made chemicals and particulate matter; animals fall, crawl or fly underground, depositing organic material as they move or when they die; and bushfires, droughts and floods alter the flow rate and chemical composition of water moving through the ground. The interconnectedness of caves and their surrounding environments is especially relevant to speleologists seeking to understand the physical processes of cave formation and development. Not only can we not see caves as they are in the present, we cannot watch them being formed. The subterranean world reveals the limits of human perception of natural phenomena in both spatial and temporal terms.

Robert A. Heinlein's science fiction novel *Citizen of the Galaxy* (1957) features a 'specialized speleologist' who knew underground 'corridors the way his tongue knew his teeth' and 'had been finding his way through them in utter blackness' with ease for years, as though the cavities and tunnels of his neighbourhood are an extension of his own body.[25] For actual speleologists, their experience of caves is more likely to reveal the fragmentary nature of specialist knowledge, than to foster the illusion that any individual can know a cave in its entirety, especially in relation to its antiquity. In short, every account of the inception and growth of caves is as much theoretical as it is factual. David Gillieson offers a useful summary of the core narrative, which unifies all accounts of cave formation without suggesting a homogenous view of the 'speleogenetic maze':

> The life history of a single cave may be envisaged as passing through a sequence of stages, not necessarily irreversibly, from an initial state of no conduits to a long inception state during which certain horizons or inhomogeneities in the rock mass act to channel water into preferred pathways. Following this a developmental phase, in which conduits form and enlarge, will persist and will respond to external factors of base level change, rock mass evolution and tectonism. Finally, in a multi-level system passages will be abandoned and will collapse, leading to a final state of no connected, enterable caves at a particular level.[26]

In broad terms, the necessary abstraction in narratives of speleohistory is a function of the incommensurability of human and geological timescales. One of the starkest reminders of the challenge caves pose to our capacity to comprehend the earth's deep time is that, once openings in rock are large enough for water to pass through, water chemistry enlarges those passages at the rate of 0.001–0.01 cm per year.

Shelfstone growing around the edges of a small cave pool. From Black Chasm Cavern, California.

Every day, tourists in limestone show caves around the world are told, for example, that the dripping stalactites before them may grow no more than the depth of a human fingernail in their lifetime. In *The Adventures of Tom Sawyer* (1876) Mark Twain succinctly explains this geological timescale in terms of human history:

> In one place near at hand, a stalagmite had been slowly growing up from the ground for ages, builded by the water-drip from a stalactite overhead. The captive had broken off the stalagmite, and upon the stump had placed a stone, wherein he had scooped a shallow hollow to catch the precious drop that fell once in every three minutes with the dreary regularity of a clock-tick – a dessert spoonful once in four and twenty hours. That drop was falling when the Pyramids were new; when Troy fell; when the foundations of Rome were laid; when Christ was crucified; when the Conqueror created the British empire; when Columbus sailed; when the massacre at Lexington was 'news.' It is falling now; it will still be falling when all these things shall

have sunk down the afternoon of history, and the twilight of tradition, and been swallowed up in the thick night of oblivion.[27]

What does it mean to study caves? When the human experience of living on the surface of the earth is so incommensurate with the temporal and spatial dimensions of the subterranean world, can anyone ever fully comprehend caves? For the British novelist and nature writer John Fowles, 'The world is not just stranger than we think; it may be stranger than we *can* think.' This conjecture seems especially insightful when read in relation to speleology. Fowles argues that the prodigious advances in science over the last century mean that to know the world 'fully, in all its scientific diversity, is already impossible'. For 'cave hunters', this is not a new idea; speleology has always recognized that even the most thorough and expert investigations of caves can only partially illuminate the planet's dark depths. Fowles concludes: 'Science strives after totality; it wants always to know more.'[28] The scientific study of caves seems instead to be founded on the principle that always wanting to know more is not necessarily to seek totality. Instead the lure of caves is always in some way a function of what humans *cannot* know – the spaces and surfaces we can neither reach nor see, the spans of time we cannot cross nor even imagine. Thus speleologists must be as invested in the certainty that caves will always be mysteries, as in their desire to know the whole truth of caves.

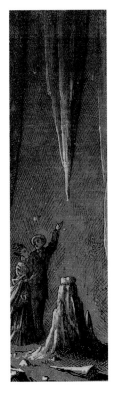

Judith Beveridge's poem, 'How to Love Bats' (1996) begins with the gentle imperative, 'Begin in a cave'. This poem uses a lesson on finding fellow feeling for bats to reflect on the limits of human knowledge, senses and perception. It offers instructions on how to imagine oneself into the body and thoughts of a creature more commonly reviled than adored. Learning to 'love bats' involves 'listen[ing] for a frequency / lower than the seep of water', 'dreaming each night of anthers', and 'practis[ing] echo-locating aerodromes'. Learning to empathize with the life of this most iconic of cave-dwellers requires going 'down on your elbows and knees', for which 'You'll need a speleologist's desire for rebirth / and a miner's paranoia of gases'. Why does a speleologist enter a cave longing to be reborn, whereas a miner ventures underground with a fear of death? And why, more particularly, are both emotions the precondition for the change of heart the poem describes? Humans, this poem suggests, do not belong in caves – they are not *our* natural homes. In order to conceive of their complexity and depth, we need to imagine ourselves otherwise or accept that in studying caves, we are also always wondering about ourselves:

> Send out rippling octaves
> into the fossils of dank caves –
> then edit these soundtracks
> with a metronome of dripping rocks, heartbeats
> and with a continuous, high-scaled wondering
> about the evolution of your own mind.[29]

Speleology, the scientific study of caves, is best approached as a holistic pursuit of knowledge and understanding, which is kept alive as much by imagination and wonder as it is by the objective hunt for facts about the earth.

'Drop after drop,' by True Williams, from the first American edition of Mark Twain's *The Adventures of Tom Sawyer* (1876).

Mum and pup, Southern Bentwing Bats, Naracoorte Caves, South Australia.

3 Troglodytes and Troglobites: Living in the Dark Zone

The English word 'troglodyte' is derived, via the Latin *trōglodyta*, from the Greek *τρώγλη* (hole) and *δύειν* (to get or go into). The noun 'troglodyte' generally refers to one of a group of people – chiefly ancient or prehistoric – who dwell in natural caves or in cave-like structures carved into cliff faces and hillsides or dug into the ground. As long ago as the fifth century BCE, the ancient Greek historian Herodotus wrote of the 'Ethiopian troglodytes' who 'eat snakes and lizards and other reptiles and speak a language like no other, but squeak like bats'.[1] And in the late tenth century CE, the Byzantine historian Leo the Deacon labelled the essentially surface-dwelling people of the Cappadocia region of present-day Turkey 'troglodytes', for their habit of living in 'caves, holes and labyrinths'.[2] In 1614 Walter Raleigh used the term to gloss a reference to regions of Africa in *The History of the World*; over the next few centuries this use of Troglodyte (with a capital 'T') to denote cave-dwelling races became standard in historical and archaeological writing. In simple terms, a troglodyte is a cave-dweller or a cave-man, but more complexly, even when the term refers to present-day peoples, it connotes the continuance of ancient practices, a return to prehistory or a mode of habitation somehow other than or antithetical to human civilization.

In phenomenological terms, caves present us with the 'opposite of the living world': 'caves are silent and static – the chaotic complexity of movements and sensory impressions in the day life outside is absent.'[3] The idea that 'cavescapes' are diametrically different to open-air landscapes is central to the history of accounts of troglodytes. For instance, in the mid-eighteenth century Carl Linnaeus determined that *Homo sapiens* (whom he also classified as *Homo diurnus* or 'day man') had a counterpart, *Homo nocturnus* or 'night man'. Following the Elder Pliny, Linnaeus named this other human species *Homo troglodytes*, and misapplied the term to albino Africans. Linnaeus based his classification of *H. troglodytes* on reports of travellers returning from Asia and Africa, and wrote that they 'lived within the boundaries of Ethiopia, in caves of Java, Ambiona, Ternate'. His description of their physical and behavioural characteristics is remarkable both in itself and for the degree to which it informed (and continues to inform) depictions of humanoid cave creatures in fantasy and science fiction:

> Body white, walks erect, less than half our size. Hair white, frizzled. Eyes orbicular: iris and pupils golden. Vision lateral, nocturnal. Life-span twenty-five years. By day hides; by night it sees, goes out, forages. Speaks in a hiss. Thinks, believes that the earth was made for it, and that sometime it will be master again, if we may believe the travellers.[4]

The confused scientific discourse about troglodytes in the eighteenth and early nineteenth centuries overlapped in important ways with religious and mythological accounts of the 'underworld' and the monstrous or supernatural people, creatures and spirits who dwell there. By the 1850s, following major discoveries of human skeletons and prehistoric artefacts in European caves, 'troglodyte' had both become more 'scientific' *and* taken on a more figurative dimension – to connote a willing or inadvertent primitivism – as it was increasingly used to label individuals who chose to live in seclusion or who were otherwise disengaged from or ignorant of the greater civilized world.

H. G. Wells looked back to Linnaeus to create a flesh-eating troglodyte species, the Morlocks, for his novel *The Time Machine*, published in 1895.[5] Wells's narrator travels to a distant future in which humanity has split into two species: peaceful

Milodón Cave, Chile.

and beautiful 'Upper-worlders' or Eloi, and degenerate, flesh-eating Morlocks. The narrator shrinks from the 'pallid bodies' of these creatures, the 'half-bleached colour of the worms and things one sees preserved in a zoological museum' and 'filthily cold to the touch'.[6] Both the Eloi and the Morlocks are a 'modification of the human type'; the surface dwellers have lived in 'too-perfect security' and slowly dwindled in 'size, strength and intelligence', but the Morlocks exhibit a more profound degeneration. Wells's descriptions clearly recall Linnaeus: the Morlocks are 'whitened Lemurs' with 'strange large greyish-red eyes'.[7] Caves are central to Wells's vision of a future in which humans have devolved and returned to the kind of prehistoric state described by Linnaeus. The link between caves and cannibalism was not new when Wells wrote *The Time Machine*; nineteenth-century archaeologists in Europe routinely misinterpreted material traces of human life in caves as evidence of prehistoric cannibalism.[8] Nor has this link faded from our geopoetic register. Caves are, for instance, a central motif in Cormac McCarthy's extraordinary dystopian novel *The Road* (2006), which opens with its protagonist waking from a dream in which he is led through a cave by his young son:

> Like pilgrims in a fable swallowed up and lost among the inward parts of some granitic beast. Deep stone flues where the water dripped and sang. Tolling in the silence the minutes of the earth and the hours and the days of it and the years without cease.[9]

The novel follows father and son as they walk through a devastated apocalyptic landscape, terrified of the cannibalistic survivors who hunt the few 'good people' remaining in a world with no life and little sunlight. Moments before his death near the end of the novel, the father dreams once again that he is in a cave, following the light of a candle held by the boy: 'in that cold corridor they had reached the point of no return which was measured from the first solely by the light they carried with them.'[10] Caves are paradoxical sites in that they signify human prehistory as much as the possibility of a way of life yet to come.

In the twentieth century, the term 'troglodyte' gained further nuance as architects interested in exploring pre-modern forms of building took it up as an adjective for a type of '*sculpted* architecture . . . cut from live rock and hollowed out'.[11] For Galena Hashhozheva, this heightened (and more positive) fascination with the idea of troglodytism was, in part, a consequence of the military rush to build underground during the world wars; by way of example, she quotes a document from the early years of the Second World War that describes a Maginot Line fort as a 'troglodyte city'.[12] Contemporary architects who look underground both recall the 'earliest prehistoric tradition of troglodytism' – even seeking a 'Palaeolithic cave "style"' – and envision a futuristic world:

For troglodytism, with its underground secrecy, carries the
germ of a different architecture and a different society (both
more horizontal than their surface counterparts) that may
be our future destiny. And who knows, architecture as we
know it may finally die out, surrendering the earth to
endless mole work.[13]

Here Hashhozheva slips between imagining humans as cave-
dwellers and picturing our gradual evolution to resemble other
subterranean mammals, such as moles, that are adapted for life
underground, but are not, strictly speaking, cave-dwellers.

The conflating of life in 'true' caves with other modes of
underground life – in artificial cavities, tunnels, burrows or soil
– is common in popular culture, and perhaps reflects that the
idea of humans living in caves is always a fantastic one. Despite
the proliferation of tales in which humans are imagined living
in the depths of caves or other subterranean hollows, there is no
archaeological evidence that humans have ever lived permanently in the truly dark zone of caves, although there are many
examples of people having taken temporary refuge in the
entrance zones of caves. Human settlements in deep hypogean
habitats are the stuff of fantasy, adventure and science fiction
and tend to be populated by relict or advanced civilizations
equipped to survive without light from the sun. Ultimately
humans are surface dwellers; we can never live fully underground but can only inhabit the threshold. The same was true
of extinct megafauna species such as cave bears, cave lions and
cave hyenas, which all made their dens or hibernated in the
entrance and twilight zones of caves, at times competing with
early humans for occupancy or food.

While humans have been dreaming of troglodytism for centuries, we have only relatively recently turned our attention to
the creatures who actually do live part or all of their lives in the
dark interiors of caves. For instance, 'It was not until 1831, when
the first troglomorphic beetle . . . was discovered in Slovenia that
caves were considered seriously as a habitat for animals.'[14] Specimens of the 'bizarre beetle, blind and unpigmented' were first

'Fauna Cavernicola'
(set of 6 stamps), Poşta
Română, 1993.

collected from Postojnska jama by Luka Čeč (who discovered
the cave in 1818);[15] the naturalist Ferdinand Schmidt produced the first scientific description of them in 1832. As late
as the early twentieth century, 'the fauna that populated
[caves] was considered to be a collection of monsters, relicts
and living fossils' and this did not really change until the century's latter half.[16] Accordingly, the term for animal species
that spend their entire lives in terrestrial subterranean habitats – 'troglobite' (and its variants 'troglobion' and
'troglobiont') – is of much more recent provenance than
'troglodyte'. While German equivalents appear in the literature in the mid-nineteenth century, it is fair to say that the
key terms of speleobiology in English were not really used

with any consistency until the twentieth century and, even today, are still in flux. David C. Culver and Tanja Pipan, the authors of *The Biology of Caves and Other Subterranean Habitats*, refer to the 'terminological jungle . . . used for ecological and evolutionary classifications of subterranean organisms'.[17] This jungle is a consequence of the relative youth of the field and the rapid pace at which it has developed in recent decades.

While the systematic study of cave life took off in the nineteenth century, there were earlier important encounters. In 1768 the Austrian naturalist Josephi Nicolai Laurenti published the first scientific description of a cave animal, the blind amphibian *Proteus anguinus*, in his manuscript *Il Dragone* (*The Dragon*). Johann Weichard von Valvasor had already mentioned this species in 1689; he wrote of animals emerging from a spring in contemporary Slovenia, claimed by locals to be the offspring of dragons.[18] Laurenti's description was of specimens he had found *outside* caves; *P. anguinus*, the 'olm' or 'human fish', was not collected from *inside* caves for another 30 years. This pale, blind salamander – since identified in over 200 subterranean sites – is the 'most famous' of deep-cave species.[19] *P. anguinus* is nicknamed the 'human fish' because of its pale skin. The irony, of course, is that the salamander's reduced pigmentation is one consequence of survival and evolution in conditions that could not sustain human life.

Pipan and Culver suggest that the 'physical appearance of *Proteus* is sufficiently bizarre that it appears to be a bridge between real and imaginary animals'.[20] In his book *Only the Nails Remain* Christopher Merrill contemplates the symbolic and cultural significance of this 'secretive creature', sometimes named as a national symbol of Slovenia:

> Though it is said the human fish descends from the dragon, photographs of it suggest a lizard lineage. Thirty centimeters long, with skin the colour of Caucasian skin, it 'tans' in the light; the farther you go into the recesses of a cave the paler the skin of the human fish. With pairs of hands, legs, and eyes, a worm-shaped body, and a flat tail, it is a figure

straight out of the dark imaginings of Henri Michaux. What it most resembles is a human fetus. It has a set of atrophied lungs. It breathes through its gills. Once it was fashionable to steal human fish and put them in caves around the world. Alas, such transplants never worked. The human fish survives only in its native place.[21]

Merrill did not see a human fish on his travels with the Slovenian writer Aleš Debeljac, who says, 'The human fish is retreating deeper into the caves closed off to tourists ... It can't stand human beings.'[22]

The cluster of images evoked by the human fish – dragon, worm, human foetus – relate to the patterns of thinking that dominate fictional *and* factual accounts of life in the dark zone of caves. The evolutionary adaptations of many categories of animals to cave living have produced some remarkable-looking animals which have attracted considerable interest despite their often inaccessible habitats. On the one hand, cavernicolous organisms and animals are radically non-human; textbooks, scholarly papers and popular science publications refer again and again to the 'bizarre morphologies' and 'strange' behaviours of troglobites and their aquatic neighbours, 'stygobites'.[23] Animals that live in perpetual darkness remind us more of beings created by J.R.R. Tolkien, Steven Spielberg or H. P. Lovecraft than anything we might encounter in the 'real world'. On the other hand, caves play a key role in our relentless anthropomorphization of the planet; their entrances are routinely described as mouths, their twisting passages as bowels and their deep hollows as wombs or brain cavities. In short, our thinking about caves is profoundly confused – they are 'other spaces' beyond the human realm, and yet we persistently treat them (and their inhabitants) as analogues for human life.

For Jim Morrison, 'In the womb we are blind cave fish.'[24] Sylvia Plath pictures 'waxy stalactites' dripping in an 'earthen womb'.[25] The narrator of Kenneth Slessor's poem 'Sleep' offers the 'huge cave' of her belly as a sanctuary, until 'Life with remorseless forceps beckon[s]'.[26] The inverse of this ubiquitous metaphor is just as common: to enter a cave is repeatedly imagined in literature and art as an experience of primal return to the mother's body or, more broadly, to human prehistory.

To venture beyond the reach of the sun's rays is frequently figured as a retreat from the norms of human existence, either through a process of devolution or estrangement. Consequently,

> Most things that characterize the world of humans (life, light, motion, colours, change, sounds and odours) do not exist in caves. This dichotomy, and the fact that caves do not have a definite termination (only points where the human body cannot pass), nourish a notion of caves as connections to realms beyond the reach of humans.[27]

One way humans make sense of our life on the planet's surface is obviously through contrast with other modes of existence – in these terms, imagining life in caves can be placed on a continuum with our fascination for life on other planets.

Perhaps the clearest embodiment of the idea that humans belong above ground is Gollum, the 'loathsome' fish-eating troglophile created by Tolkien.[28] Gollum is introduced in *The Hobbit* (1937) as 'a small slimy creature', seldom seen by locals

Postcard showing an 'olm' (*P. anguinus*) in Postojnska jama, Slovenia.

who have 'a feeling that something unpleasant [is] lurking down there at the very roots of the mountain'.[29] In *The Fellowship of the Ring* (1954), the first volume of the *Lord of the Rings* trilogy, readers learn that Gollum once belonged to a race of peaceful river folk, but long ago 'found a little cave out of which [a] dark stream ran; and he wormed his way into it like a maggot into the heart of the hills'.[30] Gollum has spent so long in the damp and the dark that he has changed irreversibly, adapting physiologically and behaviourally to the cave environment. Gollum paddles his small boat on an icy underground lake, 'looking out of his pale lamp-like eyes for blind fish, which he grab[s] with his long fingers as quick as thinking'.[31] The blockbuster film adaptations of Tolkien's trilogy exaggerate Gollum's adaptations to living underground: on the page he is 'as dark as darkness, except for two big round pale eyes in his thin face',[32] but on the screen, his skin has a pale translucency and his silent, crouching movements mimic animals adapted for survival in ecosystems where food is scarce.

Pere Alberch begins his foreword to *The Natural History of Biospeleology* by emphasizing the extreme otherness of subterranean spaces and organisms: 'Mysterious, and harsh, settings inhabited by bizarre creatures. This could be an opening sentence for a science fiction novel but it is also an apt description of subterranean environments and their faunas.' As natural environments, caves are striking examples of the unavoidable inflection of real and imagined spaces in the stories we tell about the earth, even those which make the most convincing claims of factual accuracy. Alberch explains the still hypothetical quality of prevailing ideas about cave biology as a consequence of the 'mystery' of caves. He writes, 'caves, and related underground environments, are surrounded by mystery due to their difficult access. It is not only the beauty and strangeness of the fauna they contain; just getting there represents an extraordinary achievement.' Cave biology, he concludes, combines 'science and adventure' as researchers venture into the dark looking for signs of life.[33]

To human eyes, the richest evidence of life in caves exists at the entrance zone, where the light is brightest and – depending on surface conditions – plants and animals can live in abundance. As we enter the twilight zone, where sunlight still penetrates but the walls and ceiling close in and plant and food sources become scarcer, the conditions for life as we know it get harder. To venture still deeper is to enter 'a darkness that is darker than any darkness humans normally encounter, a darkness to which our eyes cannot acclimate no matter how long one waits'.[34] Even when spotted with the aid of a headlamp, life scurries away and hides – our senses are poorly adapted both to living in caves and to observing the life that *is* there. From a human perspective, the truly dark zone might seem empty and abiotic, but a staggering array of fauna depends on this environment for survival. In the roughly 180 years since the discovery of cave-dwelling beetles in Slovenia, there has been 'slow and often erratic growth in knowledge of the organisms living in the subterranean realm, but an understanding of the vast extent of the largely inaccessible regions occupied by life beneath the earth's surface is quite recent'.[35]

Swiftlets, Twilight Cave, Mauritius.

From an ecological perspective, the very notion of a 'cave' as a distinct subterranean habitat is flawed: 'Physically, the subterranean milieu consists of extensive networks of interconnected spaces that might be filled either with air, or by fresh, brackish, or salt water.'[36] The standard distinction between caves and other subterranean cavities is based on size – microcaverns (less than 0.1 cm in width), mesocaverns (0.1–20 cm) and macrocaverns (greater than 20 cm). The term 'proper cave' was introduced by Rane L. Curl in the *Journal of Geology* in 1966 to designate natural voids large enough to permit human entry. The biologist Max Moseley contends that these distinctions are arbitrary and have little (or nothing) to do with the natural geology or ecology of caves: 'The *morphological* distinction between proper caves and smaller spaces is . . . purely anthropocentric.'[37] Importantly, thinking holistically about caves as but small parts of the underground world does not diminish their importance, but reimagines them in the context of enormous, ultimately immeasurable, ecosystems. Moseley thus proposes a redefinition of the 'larger voids that we call caves' as 'ecotones', or 'environmental and faunistic transitional regions between the surface on the one hand and the host rock fissure systems on the other', between, that is, the 'vast hypogean biome and the outside epigean world'.[38]

Moseley acknowledges that his redefinition of caves – which some will read as a demotion – is 'contentious' and that its acceptance would require a complete reversal of traditional and long-established views of the nature of caves and their relation to smaller subterranean spaces. A 'holistic ecosystems approach' to cave study and management would clearly have profound implications for biospeleology, not least by challenging the accuracy of the terminology used to describe and analyse subterranean animals.

The earliest classification systems for 'cave animals' identified darkness as the most important feature of the habitat. In 1849 a Danish naturalist, Jørgen Matthias Christian Schiødte, classified cave animals for the first time: shade animals, twilight animals, animals in the dark zone and animals living on stalactites.[39] Only

Karst landscape,
Guilin, China.

a few years later, in 1854, Ignaz Rudolf Schiner introduced a classification system that considered the 'strengths of the associations between a species and the cave environment'.[40] Given the lack of a concept of ecology (the term came into popular usage in English in the late 1870s), the limitations of these systems for twenty-first-century scientists are no great surprise. Schiner's nomenclature, revised by the Romanian zoologist Emil Racovitza in 1907, remains the most widely used today, certainly for nonspecialists, and is the basis for most systems developed since.

Racovitza's 'Essai sur les problemes biospeologiques' of 1907 marks the birth of modern biospeleology, and even though Racovitza's essay highlights narrow limestone fissures as subterranean habitats, studies of underground biology were until very recently almost entirely focused on cavities accessible to humans. The commonly used Schiner-Racovitza system describes three categories of cave-dwelling animals: troglobites (troglobionts), troglophiles and trogloxenes. Troglobites are unable to live outside the cave environment and show the most significant physical and behavioural adaptations to living in the deep cave zone. They range from thousands of identified species of troglobiotic beetles to only a handful of truly caverniculous species of fly; from 130 species of highly specialized deep cave-dwelling worms found on every continent except Antarctica to the only species of reptile adapted to spend its whole life in caves, the cave racer snake, endemic to Peninsula Malaysia and Borneo; and from widespread and numerous species of subterranean snails to only one identified species of cave clam, restricted to caves in Herzegovina and Croatia. There are troglobiotic worms, molluscs, arthropods (spiders, millipedes and crustaceans), insects, fish and salamanders, but no mammals or birds have adapted to live full-time in the deep zone. Troglophiles and trogloxenes are non-obligate cave-dwellers. The former – such as some species of cricket, spider and millipede – frequently spend their entire life cycle in caves, but are not biologically dependent on this environment and occur also in dark, humid surface habitats such as the undersides of logs or boulders. These 'cave lovers' exhibit fewer behavioural and morphological adaptations to life underground than troglobites. Trogloxenes only spend part of their life cycle in caves, returning to the surface for food; they include 'casuals' who occasionally or accidentally visit caves, 'usuals' who prefer to seek food and shelter in caves and 'habituals' whose life pattern is determined by their proximity to and their use of caves.[41] Trogloxenes include, for example, an estimated 42 per cent of species of bats, approximately 25 species of cave-nesting tropical swiftlet endemic to caves of Southeast

Cave Cricket,
Naracoorte Caves,
South Australia.

Asia and the Pacific Islands, and countless other species or 'accidentals' – such as bears, foxes and raccoons – who use caves sporadically for refuge, hunting or shelter. Some sources include humans in this category. There are, as recent scholarship in biospeleology shows, significant conceptual and practical problems associated with the models of classification that have evolved from Schiner's work. This is evident, for instance, in the fact that the prefix 'troglo-' ('cave-') became, quite early in the history of subterranean biology, untethered from its etymology and is now widely used to designate any subterranean environment.[42]

As plants need sunlight to grow, flora is restricted to the entrance zone of caves, where mosses, ferns and liverworts grow in abundance. While most cave threshold flora show little sign of adapting to the cave environment, there are some that have shown signs of adjustment. For example, a small number of mosses have developed specially shaped cells to better harness the low light found in cave entrances. One of the most interesting examples of plant life in caves is the tree roots which penetrate the ceilings of lava tubes – in Hawaii, Australia and

Composite photo of Southern Bentwing Bats, Naracoorte Caves, South Australia.

elsewhere – providing a rich food source for animals such as planthoppers and cicadas, which in turn provide food for larger cave inhabitants or visitors such as spiders and centipedes.

Well into the twentieth century scientists regarded caves as contained, finite environments and thus saw them as 'ideal natural laboratories' for the testing of key biological and ecological theories, especially in relation to processes of adaptation and evolution.[43] However caves are understood, speleobiologists have not collected a complete data set of organisms from any cave system in the world. While to the layperson's eye the truly dark zone of accessible caves may appear a sterile void, and life in mesocaverns and microcaverns be entirely invisible, subterranean environments present scientists with an apparently 'inexhaustible supply of undescribed species'.[44]

Yet in popular discourse the 'caves as islands' model persists. David Attenborough, in his narration for the BBC documentary *Planet Earth* (2006), echoes the traditional perspective:

> Many caves are like islands, cut off from the outside world and from other caves. This isolation has resulted in the evolution of some very strange creatures. They are the cave specialists – troglobytes – animals that never emerge from the cave or see daylight.[45]

Viewers are then introduced to the cave angelfish, a member of the Balitoridae (loach) family found only in waterfalls within caves in Thailand. These extraordinary animals grip cave walls with microscopic hooks on their fins, feeding on bacteria in the fast-flowing water. Attenborough speculates that they may be the 'most specialized creatures on Earth'. Viewers are invited to marvel at the 'strangeness' of cave angelfish – eyeless aquatic vertebrates who walk on walls with their fluttering white wing-like fins, their skin so pale that the colour of their internal organs makes them appear pink. The cave angelfish was filmed for the first time in the making of this documentary. The crew wore protective masks and carried oxygen monitors to cope with fluctuating oxygen and carbon dioxide levels deep in the cave, and fought to stay upright in strong water currents.[46] An anthropocentric bias is perhaps unavoidable in mainstream nature documentaries because we simply cannot comprehend the literal truth of existence for these animals. Nevertheless the depiction of cave animals in *Planet Earth* raises an important question: what are the implications of taking the concept of an 'extreme ecosystem' as our starting point for thinking about living in caves?

While it takes real effort to imagine habits and patterns of life in the perpetual dark of caves, perhaps almost as much as it does to contemplate life on other planets, the experience of living in caves is of course entirely *ordinary* to cave angelfish and other obligate cave species. For humans, Norwegian archaeologist Hein Bjartmann Bjerck writes, 'being in a cave is like being dead or unborn.' He therefore wonders whether the 'most profound embodied experience' of spending time in a cave occurs not underground, but at the moment when 'you re-enter life and the light outside: your reset senses are suddenly bombarded by all the ordinary things that filled them and your brain to a degree that borders on invisibility prior to the time spent in the dark void.'[47]

In these terms, the single most important difference between life above ground and life below ground is the absence of light. When researchers in the 1970s developed film left exposed in a cave for a week, the photographs were completely blank; the absolute darkness of caves is profoundly important to their ecology.[48] With the exception of the blue-green light of glow-worms – the maggots of a mosquito-like fly – there is no natural light in caves. Glow-worms occur only in a small number of caves in Australia and New Zealand; a chemical reaction within their bodies makes them glow and attracts flying insects to their sticky silk webs or 'snares'. This adaptation to life in the dark is so rare that some speleologists define caves as habitats 'entirely without natural illumination'.[49]

Cave spider, Sassafras Cave, Tasmania, Australia.

One of the most important – and most hotly debated – concepts for biologists seeking to understand animal life in the dark zone is 'adaptation'. In 1962 Kenneth Christiansen coined the term 'troglomorphy' to denote the morphological adaptation of organisms to subterranean habitats. This concept, first proposed by Christiansen in the journal *Spelunca*, 'redirected the emphasis [of biospeleological classification] away from ecology to the morphology of an organism'.[50] 'Troglomorphy' (and the adjective 'troglomorphic') is now a standard entry in speleological glossaries, which often list the most common adaptations to existence in the dark zone: 'loss or severe reduction of eyes and pigments, often accompanied by attenuation of the body and/or appendages'.[51] The concept of troglomorphy and related theories of evolution and adaptation begin with the assumption that cave organisms exhibit a set of similar morphological characteristics that are convergent or directly related to their evolution in similar environmental conditions. This 'neo-Darwinian paradigm' is compelling:[52] for instance, eyes serve no purpose for species that spend their entire lives in pitch darkness, so they are attenuated or absent altogether in species found in unconnected cave systems.

There are many studies in the scientific literature contrasting the phylogenesis of species in caves and surface habitats. For example, a 1995 study of cave-dwelling and spring-dwelling populations of amphipod crustacea 'found that selection intensity on eye size was in the opposite direction in the two habitats (favouring large eyes in the springs and small eyes in caves)'.[53] Increasingly, however, researchers are offering strong evidence against the principle tenets of troglomorphism. In a comprehensive survey of recent biospeleological literature, Pipan and Culver cite studies suggesting that troglomorphy is neither confined to deep caves nor as widespread in these environments as previously thought: 'No longer can we assume that subterranean habitats with troglomorphic species are primarily relatively deep in the ground and restricted to caves.'[54] Caves, in this analysis, thus lose their distinction as contained environments (analogous to 'laboratories') and are classified instead as subterranean habitats

Predjama Castle,
Slovenia.

'occurring along a continuum of several selective factors': the absence of light; the relative strength of environmental cues from the surface; the amount and variability of available nutrients; and the intensity of competition between organisms.

The behavioural adaptations of cave animals are typically explained as an evolutionary consequence of the battle to find food in an environment where there is no primary energy production (the term 'troglomorphy' is now also used to encompass morphological, physiological and behavioural adaptations). All life requires energy, and the key source of energy on Earth is sunlight. This means that almost every cave, in its depths, is an 'allobiosphere': a region where environmental 'extremes' do not permit photosynthesis and thus all energy or food sources must be imported.[55] Nutrients can be transported from the surface in percolating or flowing water, by the movement of animals or through wind or gravity. Some animals' habits appear a variation of surface behaviour. For instance, the Bornean cave racer snake spends its entire life underground. Clinging to smooth, vertical walls, it lies in ambush at the thoroughfares of bats and cave swifts where it snatches meals out of mid-air. Others behave in ways that seem more peculiar to their subterranean environment. The most obvious examples of highly specialized subterranean organisms are those found thriving in nutrient-dense bat guano piles – sometimes called 'guanobites' to signal their uniqueness.

Caves are central to the history of thought about human life on Earth. In the early decades of the nineteenth century, the first excavations of caves in Europe unearthed stone tools, pottery fragments and, most significantly, the proximate remains of humans and extinct animals. These discoveries both countered estimates of the age of the earth derived from the Bible – which dated the origins of life to 6,000 years earlier – and challenged late eighteenth-century revisions that acknowledged the evidence of extinct animals but insisted they did not co-exist with humans. As Jan F. Simek explains, 'the birth of archaeology was from the mouths of caves in Western Europe, wrapped up in one of the most momentous intellectual changes in human history: the establishment of human antiquity.'[56]

4 Cavers, Potholers and Spelunkers: Exploring Caves

'What is the strange instinct, impelling us to explore, which the sight of a cave mouth arouses?'[1]

There is no simple answer to this fundamental question posed by C.H.D. Cullingford in his 1953 introduction to *British Caving*. For cave science historian Trevor Shaw, people have faced 'the dangers and discomforts of exploring caves' for four reasons:

a) simple curiosity
b) scientific curiosity
c) commercial exploitations
d) enjoyment of a challenging sport.[2]

British cave archaeologist Edmund J. Mason explains his own attraction to searching out new territory underground in his book *Caves and Caving in Britain*: 'It was a challenge and an adventure and I appreciated the companionship of the caving fraternity . . . but there is a good deal more in caving than mere adventure.'[3] Yet despite Mason's assertion, adventure *is* the dominant trope in the history of caving and caving exploration, from William Boyd Dawkins's late nineteenth-century vision of the 'cave-hunter' recovering knowledge 'from the grasp of oblivion' to Cary J. Griffith's modern-day portrait of cavers willing to 'risk [their] lives to go where no one else has ever set foot'.[4]

We know that early humans ventured deep into caves, leaving behind them footprints and handprints, paintings and relief carvings, charcoal and the smoky residue of their torches. In 1922, when French explorer Norbert Casteret followed unknown passages deep under the Pyrenees, he found animal remains, a piece of flint 'incontestably fashioned and used by a human being', statues and carvings, the imprints of human fingers and sketches on the cave walls.[5] Interest in dark-zone cave archaeology in the United States, which dates back to the late nineteenth century, accelerated in the latter half of the twentieth century with many significant discoveries that provide evidence of ancient people exploring and using the depths of caves as burial chambers, as special purpose sites (sacred and secular) or for storage.[6] In 1988, for example, cavers mapping a cave they named Hourglass Cave in the Colorado Rocky Mountains found human skeletal remains that archaeologists were able to identify as 8,000 years old, providing evidence of the earliest known high-altitude dark-zone exploration in the Americas.[7] Similarly, speleological and geomorphological investigations in Belize have found significant remains of the

M. E. Railton, 'A typical plan of a hypothetical cave', from *British Caving: An Introduction to Speleology*, ed. C.H.D. Cullingford (1953).

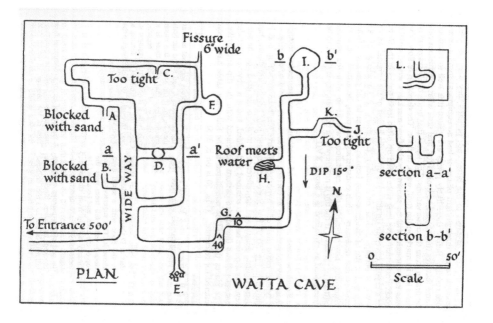

Caver, Honeycomb Cave, Tasmania, Australia.

ancient Maya that add to our knowledge of their use of caves.[8] What drove prehistoric peoples to go beyond the shadows of the cave entrance into the absolute darkness? Does it make sense to call them 'explorers'?

In many places the entrance zones of caves, like rock shelters, provided refuge and were clearly used to corral animals and store other goods. The popular notion that modern-day humans descend from the 'cave-man' imagines such sites as precursors to houses and other buildings. But there is also compelling evidence that cave openings were perceived as gateways to experiences beyond the everyday, daylight world. While traces of prehistoric journeys into cave depths can only tell us partial stories, the distinctive experience of 'being-in-the-cave' suggests that Stone Age cave visitors had something in common with today's explorers.[9] Eamon Grennan's poem 'The Cave Painters' (1991) imagines early humans pressing 'deeper into the dark' until they stand in 'an enormous womb of / flickering light and darklight'. They carry 'rushlight', pigment mixed in shells, 'crushed ore' and 'feather-tufts', and stroke images of animals and humans onto the rock walls. The poem's narrator acknowledges that we will never know why they sought out this environment to make pictures, but the final stanza insists – and rejoices – that 'it doesn't matter':

> we know
> they went with guttering rushlight
> into the dark, came to terms
> with the given world; must have had
> – as their hands moved steadily by spiderlight – one desire
> we'd recognise: they would – before going on
> beyond this border zone, this nowhere
> that is now here – leave something
> upright and bright behind them in the dark.[10]

Not only does the notion of a 'nowhere / that is now here' provide a pithy summation of the distinction between 'space' and 'place', it encapsulates the objectives and effects of human exploration of the earth. And while seeking meaning in the natural subterranean environment may be as old as human life itself, cave exploration as a distinctive activity is a relatively recent phenomenon.

A handful of scientists – notably Johann Weichard von Valvasor, Joseph Anton Nagel and Adolf Schmidl – actively explored caves for the purposes of research in the seventeenth, eighteenth and early nineteenth centuries, but the organized exploration of caves came into its own only in the late nineteenth century. The father of modern speleology is universally acknowledged to be the Frenchman Edouard-Alfred Martel, who between 1888 and 1914 explored 1,500 caves in his native France and elsewhere. His most significant explorations include the first through-crossing of the plateau de Camprieu in southern France via the underground river of the Abîme de Bramabiau on 28 June 1888, regarded by many as the birth date of modern speleology; his descent into the Gouffre de Padirac in the Lot region (now the most visited tourist cave in France) in 1889; his explorations of Marble Arch Cave in Northern Ireland and Gaping Ghyll in Yorkshire during his visit to the British Isles in 1895; and his discovery of the huge Aven Armand in the Lozère *département* in 1897.

Gaping Ghyll, at 109.7 m (360 ft), is the deepest cave shaft in Britain. Early efforts to reach the floor of the cave, notably by John Birbeck of Settle in 1842, and in 1872 by the Welshman Thomas McKenny Hughes, professor of geology at the University of Cambridge, had ended in failure, while planned attempts by Edward Calvert were repeatedly delayed, and he would not reach the bottom until 1896.[11] Ironically, 'It took a Frenchman, E. A. Martel, to make the first descent of the 360-feet-deep entrance shaft on 1 August 1895.'[12] The unlucky Calvert provides a clear account of Martel's descent:

> The ladders by which he intended to descend being only 300 feet long he attached a double rope to their top end, which again was made fast to a stout post driven into the ground. This done, he proceeded to descend from the centre

Exiting Honeycomb Cave, Tasmania.

E. A. Martel in the main shaft, Gaping Ghyll, Yorkshire, in 1895. Illustration by Lucien Rudaux.

of a goodly and awe-stricken crowd of spectators. On reaching the ledge he found the lower portion of his ladders in a heap and had to disentangle and throw them over the edge. He then continued the descent and landed on the floor of the great cavern, the sight of which impressed him greatly.[13]

The historic descent took 23 minutes. Once on the floor of the main chamber Martel drew 'an amazingly accurate sketch map of the cavern',[14] before discovering that his telephone lifeline was not working. By the time he finally managed to let the surface party know he wished to ascend, he had spent an hour and a quarter on the cavern floor, and after a 28-minute ascent he reached the surface blue with cold, which even the flask of rum he had consumed had been unable to keep at bay.

Martel's descent of Gaping Ghyll – and the extensive press coverage it attracted – provided the impetus for the establishment of many of Britain's older caving clubs (though the oldest, the Yorkshire Ramblers' Club, was formed three years before Martel's descent), and for further cave exploration in Britain, including Herbert Balch's early explorations of the Mendip karst,[15] one of the four major cave areas of Britain, along with South Wales, Derbyshire and the Northern district (parts of North Yorkshire, Lancashire, Cumbria and Durham). Martel wrote in 1896, 'Many years will elapse before [cavers] have exhausted their own "dark playground" of Great Britain.'[16]

Today British cavers wishing to explore virgin passages frequently travel abroad:

Further afield, throughout South East Asia, for example, are vast regions of unprospected limestone. Every year expeditions visit areas in China, Vietnam, Sarawak and Papua New Guinea, where huge gaping entrances await investigation. We have barely begun the exploration of the world's caves.[17]

Yet exploration by 200 British potholers over a 40-year period culminated in 2011 in the connection of more than 102 km (60 miles) of passages that stretch under Cumbria, Lancashire and Yorkshire, making the Three Counties System the longest cave network in Britain and the 22nd longest in the world, and proving that cave exploration in Britain has not yet reached a dead end, with parts of its 'dark playground' still to be discovered.

Martel made his descent of Gaping Ghyll wearing a leather cap and boots with holes drilled through the soles to allow the water to run out. Balch went underground wearing a cloth cap, an old suit and a tie. And Mason recalls wearing 'an old turned-down trilby' in his early caving days.[18] But that was set to change, as a symbiotic relationship between exploration and technical innovation developed during the twentieth century. Candles gave way to carbide lighting, which in turn has been superseded by LEDs; hemp was replaced by nylon; and old clothes were discarded in favour of boiler suits and specialized technical clothing.

The Bradford Pothole Club Winch Meet descending Gaping Ghyll, Yorkshire, 2011.

Following the First World War, two of the most prominent names in speleology were those of Robert de Joly and Norbert Casteret, who took up the mantel of their countryman, Martel, systematically exploring the caves of southwest France. Both were active cave explorers well into old age, their exploits being recorded in such works as de Joly's *Memoirs of a Speleologist* (1975) and Casteret's *Ten Years Under the Earth* (1939). De Joly, an active caver and caving administrator for over 60 years, was particularly interested in the Causses de Languedoc, where in 1935 he discovered the Aven d'Orgnac in the Ardèche region (open to the public since 1939). Earlier, in 1929, he had used a lightweight steel-cable ladder of his own invention to get to the bottom of the 'colossal' 190 m Chourum Martin in the Hautes-Alpes (which had defeated Martel, who had only been able to descend to 70 m in 1899).[19] By 1963 his friend Casteret had explored 'more than 1,200 cavities' during 'a half-century of exploration'.[20] In 1926, while caving with his wife Elisabeth (he later caved with two of his daughters), Casteret discovered what would be named the Grotte Casteret, a splendid frozen cavern in the Mont Perdu massif in the Pyrenees, which he pronounced 'a regular Jules Verne scene, but it was in life, not literature'.[21] In 1935 he reached a depth of 243 m in the Gouffre Martel in the Ariège region, then the deepest known cave in France. His legacy of exploration is supplemented by his astonishing literary legacy of 47 books on caves and caving. In the final chapter of one, *The Darkness Under the Earth* (1954), he reminds readers of the dangers of subterranean exploration: 'It must be realized that danger is always lurking underground, and that every mistake, every act of folly, is punished immediately, inevitably, and often heavily.'[22] This knowledge was something that was well understood by the great explorers who preceded and followed him.

Giant Gypsum crystals in the Naica Caves, Chihuahua, Mexico.

Over a twelve-year period which spanned the Second World War, from 1936 to 1947, a team of cavers that included Pierre Chevalier and Fernand Petzl undertook 65 expeditions, totalling 1,111 hours underground in the Dent de Crolles system near Grenoble, which at 658 m became the world's deepest explored cave at that time. Need and experiment led to new caving techniques and advances in equipment. Chevalier and Petzl invented, and were the first to use, the jointed- or scaling-pole in 1940, and they were the first cavers to use what Chevalier refers to as 'that boon to speleology',[23] the nylon rope, in 1943. They were also early pioneers of the single rope technique using mechanical rope ascenders, Brenot's 'monkeys', which Chevalier and Henri Brenot had first used underground in 1934. All these technical advances were designed with one aim in mind: to expand the possibilities of their exploration of the world's dark places. And indeed as clubs were formed and large expeditions took place in France, the world depth record was broken three times in a decade, with a depth of 1,000 m being exceeded for the first time when a team of cavers that included Petzl reached 1,122 m at the Gouffre Berger in 1956.[24] In 2012 a 200-strong European caving team led by Rémy Limagne attempted to explore and map the far reaches of this vast system, now ranked the 28th deepest cave in the world.

Whether or not he was the 'Greatest Cave Explorer Ever Known', as the epitaph on his gravestone claims, Floyd Collins is certainly a fascinating figure in the history of cave exploration in the United States. He spent his life in the Mammoth Cave region of Kentucky where, according to his brother Homer, 'he began to investigate caves seriously at age six when he wandered alone into Salts Cave only a mile from the Collins home.'[25] After years of crawling through underground passageways in the hope of finding a cave he could exploit commercially, Collins made what would be his big discovery in 1917: Crystal Cave, named for its abundant gypsum flowers, which was opened to the public in 1918. Ironically, however, it is not for his prowess as a caver that Collins is remembered, but for the way he died. On 30 January 1925 he became trapped in a narrow

Hungarian caver using
laser distance sensor in
the Abisso Sisma, Italy.
crawlway in Sand Cave, a rock pinning his foot tight. He understood the gravity of his predicament:

> He told Homer exactly how he had been caught and what
> he had discovered. 'There's a big pit down there, Homer, and
> I know it leads to a big cave. There's openings in 'n' out. But
> I got to find me a better way down to it.' With a grimace, he
> added, 'I'll shore never come this way again.'[26]

Fourteen days later he died of starvation and exposure as rescuers desperately tried to reach him, and the whole country
eagerly followed the sensational story in the media.

The motivation that drove Collins, as it has driven cave explorers before and after him, is neatly captured by Patricia Kambesis:

> In cave exploration, the initial question is very simple:
> Does it go? This is the question that hooks the cave
> explorer and drives his/her curiosity towards an answer.
> But that answer only brings more questions such as how
> far, how long, how deep?[27]

Organized exploration in the United States developed rapidly following the formation of the National Speleological Society (NSS) in 1941, set up to promote the exploration and conservation of caves. In the early days of the NSS the first person to explore a new cave was in the habit of writing his (or her) NSS membership number at the entrance and at the point of furthest penetration using soot from a carbide lamp.[28] While this method of recording exploration is no longer practised, it highlights the motivation that has driven many cavers in their exploration over the years: to enter a cavern not seen before by any human being.

American cavers have made significant contributions to subterranean exploration. The slave Stephen Bishop was responsible for much of the exploration and mapping of Mammoth Cave, where he worked as a tour guide in the mid-

A British-made Premier carbide lamp from the 1960s.

nineteenth century. Bill Cuddington, known affectionately as 'Vertical Bill', is widely regarded as the father of vertical caving (descending and ascending vertical caves on ropes) in the United States. In 1972 Patricia Crowther forced her wiry body through the Tight Spot to discover a 'real live going lead' before making possible the final connection between the Flint Ridge Cave System and Mammoth Cave, the longest known cave in the world.[29] For karst scientist William B. White, perhaps the greatest contribution American cavers have made to karst hydrology is not discovery per se, but the development and promotion, in the second half of the twentieth century, of a 'map-as-you-go' ethic for trips into unexplored caves.[30] Surveying newly discovered passages is extremely slow going and expert teams may advance no more than 46 metres per hour but, for experienced cave explorers, to rush ahead of the known map or to 'scoop' passage is a serious (and sometimes highly dangerous) transgression.

In 1980 Tom Miller and Pete Shifflett completed 'what many consider the greatest single trip in the history of American caving – and one of the most infamous'.[31] Both men had joined the team surveying Great Expectations – or Great X – in Wyoming's Bighorn Mountains 'on the strength of previous international discoveries' and set out on 17 August 1980 fully equipped with survey gear.[32] They were hoping to find a route between a newly discovered cave, Dumb Luck, and the known upper passages of Great X; success would mean a new American depth record. The surveying conditions in the cave were a 'nightmare'[33] – freezing water rushed though gruelling crawls, and squeezes lined with razor-sharp cave 'Velcro' snagged their clothing – but wind suggested that the cave continued and fuelled their determination to continue despite the very real risk of drowning, hypothermia or getting stuck in an impassable fissure. At the furthest surveyed point – a place they named Connection Falls – Miller and Shifflett abandoned the 'map-as-you-go' system and pressed forward to victory, making the connection and adding a new page to the continent's geological record. They were elated when they

'Caving adventure' phonecard issued by Telecom Australia, 1993.

reached the surface, but Idaho caver Jeb Blakely recalls, 'Tom Miller got to be a dirty word with some people . . . Him and Pete scooping Great X pissed everybody off.'[34] Their daring – if foolhardy – adventure in Great X (they named the most dangerous passage the 'Grim Crawl of Death') exemplifies the threat the earth poses to men and women intent on learning more about the places beneath its surface.

Speaking of speleology inevitably involves lamenting the loss of human life in the pursuit of knowledge. The metaphor of cave as tomb has a dreadful poignancy for scientists who are ever aware that, even with the best-laid plans, if an explorer is injured or trapped underground, a cave is a challenging, some-times impossible environment in which to effect a rescue. The difficulty of cave rescue as distinct from mountain rescue or other forms of wilderness rescue was recognized with the formation of the Cave Rescue Organisation in Yorkshire in 1935 (the world's first cave rescue organization) and the Mendip Rescue Organisation (renamed Mendip Cave Rescue in 2008) in Somerset the following year. These and other voluntary underground rescue teams in Britain are represented by the British Cave Rescue Council, which in turn is part of an international network, the Union Internationale de Spéléologie. The four-day-long rescue of Emily Davis Mobley, who broke her leg approximately two miles inside Lechuguilla Cave in New Mexico in 1991, is a celebrated and well-documented success story. Another successful operation was mounted in June 2012 in the vertical cave system of Kita Gaćešina in Croatia, where caver Marijan Marović was rescued after sustaining a lumbar spine injury following a fall at -483 m, caused by the failure of an anchor plate. The two-day drama involved 114 rescuers from sixteen Croatian Mountain Rescue Service stations. Other accidents in caves have been fatal. In the Gouffre Berger alone there have been six fatalities in recent years, five of them, including Englishwoman Nicole Dollimore and Hungarian Istvan Torda who both died in 1996, due to violent flooding in the cave that was once thought the deepest in the world.

James M. Tabor's book *Blind Descent* tells the extraordinary and harrowing tale of two twenty-first-century cave explorers' efforts to achieve 'the last great terrestrial discovery . . . the deepest cave on earth'.[35] In 2004 the American explorer Bill Stone led an expedition to Cheve Cave in southern Mexico, determined to penetrate deeper than anyone had ever been before. In the same year the Ukrainian Alexander Klimchouk looked towards Krubera, 'a freezing nightmare of a supercave in the Republic of Georgia'.[36] Tabor coined the term 'supercave' – which he also uses in his adventure novel *The Deep Zone* (2012) – to name the biggest, deepest caves on earth:

> If you imagine Mount Everest in reverse, that's a really good image to start with. For one thing, they're immensely deep. Krubera, the great cave in Georgia, is 7,000 vertical feet deep . . . so seven Empire State buildings . . . But an equally

significant dimension is the length. It's almost nine miles from the mouth of the cave down to its terminus. So it would take the explorers a week to get down to the place where exploration was actually occurring. They would spend seven to ten days exploring there, and then it would take them a week to get out. So these expeditions would spend up to a month underground.[37]

Tony Brown, Northern Boggarts, negotiating the Portcullis duck in Disappointment Pot, one of the many entrances to the Gaping Ghyll system in Yorkshire.

Caves for many twenty-first-century explorers provide the last opportunity for exploration and original discovery, as the 'subterranean world' is the 'sole remaining realm that can be experienced only firsthand, by direct human presence'.[38] This is a view that seems to unify devotees to cave exploration – from committed weekend cavers to the leaders of large-scale international expeditions.

Speaking on local radio in Tasmania, the state with the longest and deepest caves in Australia, caver Jason Gardner explained his love of underground exploration: 'There's not many places on the planet you could say you were the first

Entrance zone, Honey-comb Cave, Tasmania, Australia.

person to actually go.'[39] While such statements are common in tales of cave exploration, they are ubiquitous in accounts of cave diving – unquestionably the most dangerous way to explore the earth's wild places. The history of cave diving for exploration begins with Casteret's celebrated free dive through a 'sump' (a section of cave passage where the ceiling drops below water level) in a cave in the Pyrenees near the village of Montespan. In 1922 villagers led Casteret to the base of a hill where a stream flowed from the rock and he slid 'through a hole the size of a man's body' to emerge in a passage about

3–3.5 m wide and half as high. After wading through the
stream for around 56 m, Casteret found himself in a 'discour-
aging spot' where the cave roof disappeared below the water,
and where the celebrated cave scientist René Gabriel Jeannel
had previously been forced to stop:

> With the water reaching to my shoulders, in this current
> which flowed through a submerged tunnel, I thought in the
> meantime of how senseless it might prove to persevere alone
> in an enterprise so dangerous.
>
> What were the probabilities?
>
> For an indefinite distance ahead of me I might find the
> stream touching the roof as it did at the point of egress; I
> might be barred by a rocky cul-de-sac; reach a subterranean
> lake; come to a precipice, to a pocket of poisonous air, or to a
> pile of branches carried down by the waters, and which hold
> danger or death in their tangled arms.
>
> After having weighed these diverse possibilities in the
> impressive silence of my solitude, I decided to push on into
> the unknown, to pass, if possible, this barrier which the
> combination of water and rock seemed to render inviolable.[40]

Casteret took a deep breath (enough air to last two minutes) and
sank into the water, keeping his hand on the submerged roof.
Miraculously, he found air and emerged in absolute darkness.
Casteret survived this dive and returned the following morning
with candles and matches wrapped in his waterproof bathing
cap, determined to venture further into the icy, black water.
Casteret explained that 'the excitement and the lure of the
unknown' drove him to keep pushing forwards.[41]

Diving in water-filled subterranean passages fits the standard definition of 'extreme sports': 'independent sports where
the most likely outcome of a mismanaged mistake or accident
is death'.[42] Contrary to the common perception of extreme
sports, narratives of cave diving do not suggest that divers who
venture into the dark are seeking the thrill of risk-taking. For
diving instructor Edrich Smook, diving is

not an adrenaline sport. The appeal is more profound. In a cave, during a challenging dive, the most minor act becomes crucial; simply tying a knot on a line is absorbing. You are completely in the moment. You are living fully.[43]

Smook is quoted in Phillip Finch's book *Raising the Dead*, which tells the story of Australian Dave Shaw's daring and doomed attempt to retrieve the body of a diver, Deon Dreyer, from the bottom of Boesmansgat (Bushman's Hole), South Africa, where it had lain for over a decade. On 8 January 2005, Shaw died at a depth of 270 m, connected to Dreyer's headless body by the taut cave line in which he had become entangled. His diving partner, Don Shirley, who only just escaped the dive with his own life, has said, 'I don't see a cave as a nasty place and neither did Dave. A cave is where we lived. It's where life happened.'[44] From another perspective, Shaw's death – every desperate second recorded by a camera mounted on his helmet – highlights the fundamental incompatibility of the human body with deep water-filled caves, which may be part of the attraction of cave diving.

For speleologists working today, advances in diving technology mean that data and material samples which once seemed forever beyond their reach are becoming increasingly accessible; however, once a subterranean environment fills with water it becomes exponentially more dangerous to humans. In 2007 a Belgrade University lecturer and three of his students, all members of a Serbian speleological association, died of suffocation while diving in water-filled sections of Ravanica Cave. Two members of a cave-diving team, Wes Skiles and Agnes Milowka, who in 2008 ventured into the 'scientific trove' of the blue holes of the Bahamas on a research expedition funded by National Geographic, have since died in diving accidents. The team of divers on the Blue Hole Expedition had to swim through a toxic layer of hydrogen sulfide to reach the 'living laboratories' of dozens of inland flooded caves and to collect material samples and data which promised to enrich scientists' 'understanding of everything from geology and water chemistry to biology,

Jill Heinerth, 'Two highly experienced rebreather divers approach the Grim Reaper sign at Ginnie Springs inside Devil's Ear Spring, Florida. These signs are meant to warn untrained divers about the hazards of diving in underwater caves.'

paleontology, archaeology, and even astrobiology – the study of life in the universe'.[45] In an interview broadcast on Australia's SBS Radio in 2010, Milowka spoke of the excitement of working alongside the scientists in the Bahamas, collecting the samples they needed from deep inside underwater caves:

> You can find skeletons of animals that have been extinct for thousands of years and yet the fossils remain preserved in perfect condition inside the cave. The fossils look like they have fallen in yesterday but really they are over 3,000 years old. It's quite incredible.

She also spoke candidly about the dangers of cave diving:

> Unfortunately there are risks; in every extreme sport there are dangers. It doesn't always work out but you do everything possible to not only do that one dive, but to keep on diving over many years. That's what it's all about after all, longevity. You have to dive safely but live as if everyday is going to be your last.[46]

Sheck Exley – regarded by his peers as one of the greatest cave divers ever, and in 1994, the year of his death, the holder of the record for the deepest dive – summed up the lure of cave diving in his autobiography, *Caverns Measureless to Man*:

> In one way, a cave explorer's thrill is greater than that of undersea explorers or astronauts: in this day of telescopes, space probes, sonic probes, and remote cameras, they can study where they are going ahead of time; cave explorers go into the unknown. Moreover, unlike an explorer of air-filled caves, a cave diver is rarely worried by the nagging suspicion that a torch-bearing prehistoric Indian might have been there before him: the technology for exploring underwater caves is scarcely three decades old.[47]

The history of cave diving – which Martyn Farr, one of Britain's leading cave divers, allows in his fascinating introduction to the sport is 'extreme behaviour'[48] – *can* be told as an adrenaline-filled tale of campaigns to push deeper and further into the earth but it can also be told as a sober story of the collective effort to reduce risk through better training, improved safety protocols and advancements in technology. Almost all dedicated and experienced cave divers have recovered the bodies of dead friends or come terrifyingly close to death themselves. In the words of Exley, there is no escaping the 'routine but grim matters of survival'.[49]

The ability of cave divers to penetrate deeper and further into underwater caves has always been dependent on new technologies as well as human potential. In the future the desire of cavers to negotiate tighter, deeper and longer passages will be increasingly reliant on fresh technological innovations (in closed circuit rebreathers, decompression techniques, scooters and so on) that must inevitably include the use of miniature robots or other non-human exploration techniques. For those areas that remain within the orbit of human cavers – albeit with the aid of ongoing technological advances – the risks and the rewards will increase side by side. But the lure of exploring 'territory never before seen by man' will prevail.[50]

5 Monsters and Magic: Caves in Mythology and Folklore

More than any other single landscape feature, caves play a significant role in mythologies and folklores from around the globe. In ancient mythologies, in popular folklore and in indigenous traditions they are places of fancy and the imagination; yet strangely these predominantly fantastic stories are not untouched by the science of geology or geological history. In countless mythological tales caves are dark mysterious places inhabited by gods, giants, dragons and other supernatural or malevolent spirits. They are containers for spiritual stories; they are places of birth and burial, the homes of ancestors and the resting places of the souls of the dead; they are associated with fertility and sacrifice; and they provide passage to the underworld. In Greek mythology, Zeus grew up in a cave; the twin founders of Rome, Romulus and Remus, were suckled by a she-wolf in the cave of Lupercal; according to Arthurian legend, the wizard Merlin lived in a cave beneath Tintagel Castle, where he performed his magic; in Maori mythology the dark places inhabited by taniwha include caves; and in Native American and Australian Aboriginal stories caves are associated with creation myths and are the homes of mythical beings. As Michael Ray Taylor succinctly puts it, 'Cave images and anecdotes permeate world mythology.'[1]

Commonly, caves in the world's ancient mythologies are the abode of gods, demons or other mythological creatures. Zeus, the most powerful of the Greek gods (Jupiter is the Roman equivalent), was born in a cave on the slopes of Mount Ida in Crete where his mother, Rhea, hid him from his father, Cronus, who, having learnt that he was destined to be overthrown by his son, had swallowed each of his children as they were born. Zeus eventually freed his siblings and overthrew his father, banishing him to the infernal regions. Two caves on Crete are promoted as the place of Zeus' birth: the Idaian Cave and Cave of Psychro (or the Dictaean Cave). Both were important places of worship during the Minoan period and have been extensively excavated, revealing votive offerings and other artefacts which are now on display in museums around the world including the Heraklion Archaeological Museum on Crete, the Ashmolean Museum in Oxford and the Louvre in Paris. Another Cretan cave is said to be the birthplace of Eileithyia, the goddess of childbirth and midwifery (who is closely associated with Artemis). In Roman mythology Somnus, the god of sleep (Hypnos in Greek mythology), resides in a dark cave that the sun never penetrates, its entrance curtained by poppies and other hypnotic plants. Hermes, the god of travellers, was born in a cave on Mount Cyllene, while Aeolos, the keeper of the winds in Greek mythology, kept his winds locked away in a cave, only letting them out when instructed by the gods. Many other ancient deities also resided in caves and grottoes.

The many-headed serpent Hydra lived in a cave, as did the serpent Python. The snake-haired Medusa lived in the secret Cave of the Gorgons, while both Pindar and Aeschylus make reference to the monstrous Typhon, 'the hundred-headed, native of the Cilician caves'.[2] Cacus, a fire-breathing giant of Roman mythology, is said to have dwelt in a cave on the Palatine Hill in Italy, which became the site of Rome. His grisly mountain abode is described by Virgil in Book 8 of the *Aeneid*:

... take a look at this cliff, overhung by its uppermost rock-ledge;
   Note where its mass is extensively shattered and where an abandoned
   Cave-dwelling stands, though the overhang's fall wrought enormous destruction
   This was at one time a cave stretching far back under the hillside,

Corycian Cave entrance, Greece.

Hiding within it, where rays of the sun couldn't enter, the fearsome
    Visage of subhuman Cacus. The groundsoil was warmed into humus
    Constantly freshened with slaughter; and nailed with pride at the entrance
    Hung human heads, each face decomposing grimly to greyness.[3]

Postcard: mid-20th century visitors to Waitomo Cave, New Zealand.

A renowned robber and the demon-son of Vulcan, Cacus was killed in a fierce battle by Hercules for stealing some of his prize cattle. Significantly this passage dating from the first century BCE highlights the way mythological stories frequently interact with geology: here the great Roman poet foregrounds such geological events as breakdowns, and separates the twilight and dark zones of the cave.

Cacus and the Gorgon Medusa are both evoked by the English Enlightenment philosopher Thomas Hobbes in his poem 'De Mirabilibus Pecci', written following his tour of the Peak District in 1626 (published in Latin in 1636 and in an English translation by 'a Person of Quality' in 1678) when he describes Poole's Cavern, the hideout of another legendary robber:

> Pool was a famous thief, and as we're told
> Equal to *Cacus*, and perchance as old.
> Shrowded within his darksome hid retrieve
> By spoils of those he robb'd, he us'd to live,
> And towards his den poor travellers deceive;
>
> . . .
>
> This Cave by *Gorgon* with her snaky hair
> You'd think was first possest; so all things there
> Turn'd into Stone for nothing does appear
> That is not Rock. What from the ceiling high
> Like hams of *Bacon* pendulous you spy,
> Will scarce yield to the teeth; stone they are both.
> That is no Lyon mounts his main so rough,
> And sets as a fierce tenant o' th' dark den,
> But a meer yellow Stone.
>
> . . .
>
> Our lights persuade us now grown tow'rds decay,
> To haste from the Caves labarinth away.
> But turning first on the left hand, behold
> The bed-chamber of *Pool* the robber bold
> All of plain Stone, ne're water'd with the dew,
> Furnish'd with bed and chamber-pot we view.[4]

In recounting the legend of Pool the robber Hobbes appears to offer an implicit rejection of the appropriation of cave geology by mythology and folklore. Instead he presents his readers with a subtle pro-science description of the rogue's den, while still recognizing the importance of human perspective in the interpretation of caves. Hobbes displays a surprisingly complex understanding of the solution processes which have created the geological formations he highlights: a flitch of bacon, stalactites and stalagmites, flowstone and a rim pool serving as a chamber pot!

The most famous caves in Western mythology must be those found in Homer's epic poem the *Odyssey*, said to date

from the eighth century BCE, which records the adventures of
Odysseus (Ulysses) as he makes his way home to Ithaca after
the battle of Troy. Of the many caves that feature in this major
early work of Western literature, the caves of the Cyclops
Polyphemus, the monstrous Scylla and the enchanting Calypso
are the best known.

Early in their journey home Odysseus lands on an island
and with twelve of his men enters a cave which is the home of
the giant Cyclops Polyphemus in search of food. The cave of
plenty is vividly described by Homer as Odysseus and his men
marvel at the Cyclops' cave:

> So we explored his den, gazing wide-eyed at it all,
> The large flat racks loaded with drying cheeses,
> The folds crowded with young lambs and kids,
> Split into three groups – here the spring born,
> Here mid-yearlings, here the fresh sucklings
> Off to the side – each sort was penned apart.[5]

When the Cyclops returns and discovers Odysseus and his men
in his cave he blocks the entrance with an immense stone, and
immediately eats two of the sailors. After six of the sailors have
been devoured Odysseus effects an escape by blinding the sleep-
ing giant and then riding out of the cave tied to the undersides
of Polyphemus' sheep as he lets them out to graze.

While the Cyclops' cave is both a comfortable abode and a
place of cannibal atrocity, the lair of the six-headed monster
Scylla is a 'fog-bound cavern', a 'yawning cave', a 'terrifying pit'.
Odysseus is warned to steer his ship past this 'realm of death
and darkness' as he negotiates the narrow strait between the
whirlpool of Charybdis and the cliffs where Scylla is 'Holed up
in the cavern's bowels from her waist down'.[6] Odysseus does pass
between these two great monsters, but at the cost of Scylla swal-
lowing another six of his men. Again the cave is presented as a
place of horror and death. In apparent contrast, the spacious
cave of the nymph Calypso is a place of intimate pleasure, where
'Calypso the lustrous goddess tried to hold [Odysseus] back, /

Detail of the Zeus
Cavern, Cave of
Psychro, Crete.

Deep in her arching caverns, craving [him] for a husband.'[7] This
cave is both a prison that delays Odysseus' journey home by a
further seven years until Zeus orders his release, and a site of
rebirth, from which he emerges to continue his journey.

Caves are also 'a source of wisdom and knowledge' in
mythology, as Chris Tolan-Smith reminds us.[8] Various sibyls
(or prophetesses), including the Cumaean sibyl and the Del-
phic sibyl, delivered their prophecies in caves. The most
celebrated is the Cumaean sibyl who resided in a cave near

Engraved for The Complete English Traveller.

'View of that part of the Peak of Derby, commonly called the **Devil's A–se**; – and another part, called **Pool's Hole**.

Naples, and wrote her prophecies on oak leaves which she would arrange inside the entrance of her cave. In Book VI of the *Aeneid*, Virgil's Aeneas visits the Cumaean sibyl to learn how to enter Hades and return alive. In her third novel, *The Last Man* (1826), Mary Shelley uses the Cumaean sibyl as a framing device for the story narrated by Lionel Verney at the end of the twenty-first century. The narrator of Shelley's introduction describes in detail how she and her companion 'entered the gloomy cavern of the Cumaean Sibyl'. They make their way through 'murky subterranean passages', 'a natural archway, leading to a second gallery', 'a small opening', several tight passages, and a succession of ascents until they arrive 'at a wide cavern with an arched dome-like roof'. Here they discover a trove of sibylline leaves from which the narrative that follows is drawn.[9] Moving forward to the middle of the twentieth century, the 'mouthy cave' and 'dumb grottoes' meld the notion of the cave speaking with the prophecies of the sibyl in Geoffrey Hill's poem 'After Cumae' (1958).[10]

The Corycian Cave on Mount Parnassus, also known as Pan's Cave, is sacred to both the nymph Corycia and to Pan. The

'View of that part of the Peak of Derby, commonly called the *Devil's A–se*; – and another part, called *Pool's Hole*', engraved for *The Complete English Traveller* (1771).

Greek historian, geographer and philosopher Strabo mentions the cave, located between Delphi and Parnassus, in the ninth book of his seventeen-volume *Geographica.* The stalactites and stalagmites in this enormous cavern are described by the Roman naturalist Pliny the Elder in his *Natural History*, published around 77–9 CE:

> In the caverns of Mount Corycus, the drops of water that trickle down the rocks become hard in the form of stone. At Mieta, too, in Macedonia, the water petrifies as it hangs from the vaulted roofs of the rocks; but at Corycus it is only when it has fallen that it becomes hard.[11]

And again a hundred years later the Greek geographer Pausanias describes the interior of the Corycian Cave in the tenth book of his travelogue, *Description of Greece*:

Jacob Jordaens, *Odysseus in the Cave of Polyphemus, c.* 1635, oil on canvas.

> the Corycian cave exceeds in size those I have mentioned, and it is possible to make one's way through the greater part of it even without lights. The roof stands at a sufficient

'Silver Cave triptych', Silver Cave, Yangshuo County, China.

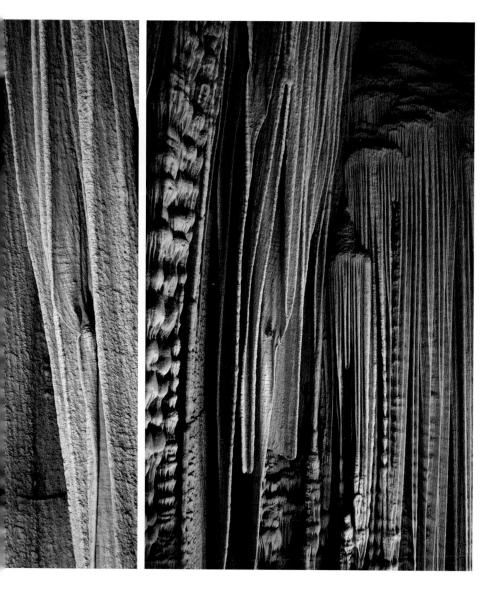

Mayan archaeological
site, Actun Tunichil
Muknal, Belize.

height from the floor, and water, rising in part from springs
but still more dripping from the roof, has made clearly
visible the marks of drops on the floor throughout the cave.[12]

These caves are described by Strabo, Pliny and Pausanias less
for their geology than for their mythological associations. For
these writers the interest of the caves is elevated above geology
by mythology.

Caves are home, too, to many other creatures that have
figured in the mythology and legends of the world. Dwarves,
which feature prominently in Germanic and Scandinavian legends, live in caves and the deep recesses of the earth, as do the
dragons in European folklore, from Poland to Wales, despite
generally having wings. The Polish Wawel dragon, for example,
lived in caves on the Vistula river bank outside Krakow, and the
Mabinogion recounts the imprisonment of two dragons beneath
Dinas Emrys in Snowdonia. Gnomes, popular in modern fantasy literature, are generally presented as living in caves or
underground, as in C. S. Lewis's *The Chronicles of Narnia* (1949–
54), where the gnomes or 'Earthmen' live in a series of
subterranean caverns known as Underland. Goblins, too, frequently inhabit underground lairs, as do trolls in Norse and
Scandinavian mythology, while the South African Grootslang, a
legendary serpent-like creature, dwells in a deep cave in the
mountainous Richterveld.

Caves also have a significant presence in Celtic mythologies. They are entrances to the Otherworld, the Celtic realm
of the dead; the domain of fairies; and home to demons and
heroes. In Ireland the Cave of Cruachan, or Oweynagat (the
Cave of the Cats), which today can be entered through a tiny
souterrain in a field in County Roscommon, is associated with
Queen Maeve of Connacht and the Morrígan, the Irish God-
dess of Battle, and appears in numerous Irish legends including
'Bricriu's Feast', from the *Ulster Cycle*, and 'The Adventures of
Nera in the Otherworld', in which the warrior Nera enters the
Otherworld through Oweynagat. The huge, three-chambered
Dunmore Cave near Kilkenny, with its imposing entrance –

described in folklore as 'the mouth of a huge beast with ten thousand teeth above his head and as many under his feet',[13] and known as the darkest place in Ireland – was home to the legendary Luchtigern, the Mouse-Lord who was slain by a monster cat. The cave, the site of a Viking massacre in 928 CE, is now a show cave where visitors can see the Market Cross, a large dripstone pillar, the pure calcite formations of the Town Hall Chamber and a bat colony. The folklore of the Isle of Man has the cughtagh, a relative of the Scottish shape-shifting ciuthach, a malicious spirit who dwells in caves and caverns near the sea, and 'whose voice was the soughing of the wavelets'.[14]

As well as the fantastic and mythological creatures associated with the subterranean, folklore has tales of quasi-historical figures linked to caves. Robin Hood, perhaps the most famous of all legendary outlaws, is said to have taken refuge on several occasions in a cave, and nowadays various caves, each supposedly the site of his temporary hide-out, bear his name. The most noteworthy is at Creswell Crags, on the Derbyshire–Nottinghamshire border. This cave, which has four main chambers linked by short passages, may not have sheltered Robin Hood, but it has clearly been home to others. Archaeological excavations carried out in the nineteenth and twentieth centuries have unearthed a wide range of stone tools and animal bones dating as far back as Neanderthal times. According to Arthurian legend, King Arthur was buried on the Isle of Avalon; however, there is also a less well-known legend that claims King Arthur and his knights are resting in a mystical cave where they will remain until the time Britain needs them most. Again several sites are linked to this legend, but the one with the greatest claim is King Arthur's Cave 'situated at the foot of a low cliff at the north western end of Lord's Wood on the hill of Great Doward at Whitchurch near the River Wye', which 'consists of a broad entrance platform, a double interconnected entrance and two main chambers'.[15]

In Native American mythology the Hopi have a creation story which describes the tribe emerging through a series of underworlds or caves.[16] Navajo mythology shares a similar creation story. Local Miwok living around Moaning Cavern (or Samwel Cave) in Calaveras County, California, have a legend about Yayali, a rock giant who lives in the depths of the large vertical chamber and eats those he lures to the entrance with his moaning sound. Caves are even more deeply rooted in the mythology of the indigenous peoples of Mesoamerica. As Nicholas J. Saunders notes, 'the Aztecs had many myths concerning caves as entrances to the underworld, as places where time and humanity began, and as "places of emergence."'[17] Similarly, in Mayan mythology caves were entrances to the underworld, Xibalba – 'a dripping vaulted house of rock' in Allen Ginsberg's poem 'Siesta in Xbalba'.[18] Many of the caves believed by the ancient Maya to be portals to Xibalba have been explored by archaeologists; among these is Actun Tunichil Muknal (the Cave of the Stone Sepulchre) in Belize, a sacrificial chamber where human remains have been found, along with pottery vessels permanently embedded in the cave's formations. There are also many myths and legends surrounding the blue holes of the Bahamas. The most popular is the legend of the half-squid, half-shark sea monster, Lusca, that dwells in the holes and sucks victims down to be devoured in the watery deep. (The extremely strong currents that oscillate with the tide in the blue holes of the Bahamas are probably the basis of this particular myth.)

In Maori mythology caves are home to many fabulous creatures including the giant bird-woman Kurangaituku; the dog-headed monster Kopuwai; the yellow-haired, white-skinned Karitehe, a fairy tribe who lived in the Kauhoehoe Caves; and, of course, the taniwha. The best-known creature of Maori legend, the taniwha can be either a protector or predator of the local people. Araiteuru is a cave-dwelling taniwha associated with the Hokianga Harbour; Rapanui and Kaiwhare are taniwha from Manukau Harbour and Owheao is a taniwha from the Taupo district. Caves can also be tapu (sacred) places for Maori, where high-ranking people were buried.[19]

In other Polynesian mythology the Makua Cave, on the Hawaiian island of Oahu, also known as Kaneana Cave, is named after the god Kane, the god of creation, and legend has

69. Bride's Jewels, Ruakuri Caves, N.Z

it that the cave is the womb from which humankind was born. Another story is that the cave was the home of the shark-man of Kaneana, who would drag his victims into the cave to devour them.

Postcard: Bride's Jewels, Ruakuri Caves, New Zealand.

The pattern continues in Australia where, as Ian D. Clark explains,

> Caves and sink holes featured prominently in the lives of Aboriginal people – they were often believed to be the abode of malevolent creatures and spirits and some were associated with important ancestral heroes, and traditional harming practices. Some were important in the after death movement of souls to their resting places.[20]

In the tribal legends of the Gunai people from the Gippsland area of Victoria, caves are believed to be inhabited by two dreamtime creatures, the Nargun and the Nyol. The half-human, half-stone Nargun is a fierce creature that haunts the bush, dragging passers-by into his cave and killing them. Both the Nargun and the mischievous cave-dwelling Nyols feature in

Patricia Wrightson's award-winning children's novel *The Nargun and the Stars* (1973). In *Rock Art of the Dreamtime* Josephine Flood recounts the Mirning belief that 'a huge hideous snake called Jeedara, or Ganba, lived in the caves and blowholes on the Nullabor Plain, and ate anyone who came into his territory.'[21] In the stories of the Wardandi people of Western Australia, Ngilgi Cave was once the home of the evil spirit Wolgine who was defeated in battle and banished from his cave by the good spirit Ngilgi. Interestingly the legend, which tells of the collapse of the tunnel entrance during the fierce battle, and Wolgine being driven up through the earth to form another entrance, is mirrored by the geological history of the cave.

From the mythological stories of ancient Greece and Rome, to the dreamtime stories of Australia's Aboriginal people, caves feature strongly in fabulous tales from around the world. In all these legends caves are magical, extraordinary places, home to gods and monsters, providing passages to and from other worlds. They are dark, deep places, home to the unfamiliar and the unexpected, but never quite out of touch with the human encounter zone.

6 Visually Rendered: The Art of Caves

Cave art challenges the geological versus human (permanent versus impermanent) binary opposition; like geological formations, cave art endures. Caves are our oldest art galleries; the world's oldest-known paintings are found on the walls and occasionally on the ceilings of caves. Among the most famous of these are the paintings found in the cave of Altamira near Santander in Spain, 'nicknamed the Sistine Chapel of Cave Art',[1] and the cave of Lascaux near Montignac in southern France, both of which contain paintings dating back over 15,000 years, and the cave of Chauvet, in the Ardèche region of southern France, which contains cave art from a staggering 30,000 years ago.

The roof of the main chamber in the Altamira cave (which provided the inspiration for the song 'The Caves of Altamira' on the 1976 album *The Royal Scam* by the American jazz-rock band Steely Dan) is covered with paintings, mostly of bison, but also wild boars, horses, deer and other figures. The walls and ceilings of the Lascaux cave are decorated with 600 paintings and 1,500 engravings, again mostly of animals, including bison, aurochs, horses, deer and cats. To protect the paintings from further damage caused by years of heavy visitor traffic, the artificial lighting and the ensuing growth of algae, bacteria and crystals, both caves have been closed to the public with facsimile caves built nearby – Lascaux II and Altamira II – affording visitors a vivid impression of both the prehistoric artwork and the original grottoes themselves. The Chauvet cave, discovered in 1994,

Bison in the caves at
Altamira, Spain.

has never been open to the public, though one can see the astonishing cave art – thirteen species of animals including
mammoths, bears, lions and the great panel of horses – as well
as the speleothems of the vast underground caverns, in Werner
Herzog's 3D film *Cave of Forgotten Dreams* (2010). Not only did
the caves provide a canvas for the prehistoric artists, most commonly using red or black pigments, but they also became an
intimate part of the art itself, the natural relief lending form and
feature to the work: a bison's shoulder, a lion's pelvis. As John
Canady explains, 'Where the natural rock is either convex or
concave in form suggesting an animal's body or a portion of it,
the cave artist frequently capitalized on this form as a beginning
and adapted his drawing to its contours.'[2] By using the cave's
natural features in this way the cave artist perfectly merged the
human art form and the geological formations.

Cave art is not only found in Europe; indeed, it is a feature
of every continent except Antarctica. In Africa cave art has been
found from the Sahara to South Africa, from the swimming
figures of the Cave of Swimmers in Egypt to the human and
animal figures executed by the San people in South Africa. In

Asia there are rock paintings in caves or shelters in India, Sri Lanka, Burma, Thailand, Malaysia and Indonesia. The paintings in the numerous Bhimbetka rock shelters in India's Madhya Pradesh state, described in the Lonely Planet guide as 'a must-see',[3] date back to up to 12,000 years and depict scenes from the lives of the cave-dwellers, as well as animals including bison. Animal and human subjects are represented in rock paintings dating back 11,000 years on the walls of the Neolithic Padah-Lin Caves in Burma's Shan state. In Sri Lanka, exquisite portraits of women painted in the fifth century CE survive on the walls of a sheltered gallery part way up the ancient Sigiriya rock fortress. In North America cave art sites are spread across the western states, the Southwest, the Midwest and the southeastern states. Cave art in the western United States 'typically occurs in basalt formations' such as Owl Cave in Washington which 'houses paintings in an 18 m diagonal basalt fissure'.[4] (An Owl Cave in the fictional Ghostwood National Forest featured

Bhimbetka rock shelters, Madhya Pradesh, India.

Cueva de las Manos, Santa Cruz, Argentina.

in three episodes of the second season of *Twin Peaks*, screened in 1991.) Exploration of Mud Glyph Cave in Tennessee (in the 1980s) and other glyph caves in the southern Appalachians 'revealed the dark zone to be the scene of prehistoric ceremonial activity' and suggested 'that ceremonial decoration of cave walls in the southeastern United States was practiced for several thousand years, from the Late Archaic through the early historic periods'.[5] In Central America Mayan cave paintings have been found in the Yucatán, Mexico, and in the Caribbean a significant concentration of cave art from the last two millennia can be found in Cuba and the Dominican Republic. In South America there are prehistoric cave paintings, principally near entrances, in both Brazil and Argentina dating from around 9000 BCE. The Cave of the Hands (Cueva de las Manos) in Argentina – named for the many stencilled images of hands that can be seen on the walls along with images of humans and animals, and geometrical drawings – contains the oldest-known

Engravings in Malangine Cave, Mount Gambier, South Australia.

cave paintings in South America. The cave art in the New World, however, 'does not approach the antiquity of European or Australian examples'.[6]

Evidence of cave art in Australia can be traced across the length and breadth of the country, from Arnhem Land in the far north, to Tasmania in the south, and from Western Australia's Kimberley to the Chillagoe region of north Queensland. The main cave petroglyph sites occur in four karst areas across southern Australia: near Perth, the Nullarbor Plain, Mount Gambier and Buchan.[7] Relatively speaking, in world terms Australia has few caves, and only a small corpus of cave art. Koonalda Cave is a large, crater-like limestone sinkhole on the South Australian part of the Nullarbor Plain. It contains 'abundant "digital flutings" (lines made with fingers) on the ceiling and walls, in total darkness, hundreds of metres inside', which Josephine Flood ranks 'one of the most remarkable discoveries in Australia'.[8] The major concentration of cave art in Australia is found in the Mount Gambier region of South Australia where the art is mostly non-figurative, and falls into three distinct chronological phases: finger fluting, simple geometric motifs and shallow engravings.[9] Finger fluting, the earliest and most common style, is in evidence in the majority of caves in the Mount Gambier region, as well as elsewhere on the continent. The second tradition, called Karake after the cave where it was first seen, is 'characterized by deeply engraved and weathered circles',[10] and has been found only in limestone caves in the Mount Gambier region. One of the best examples of this style of art is the 'gallery' in Paroong Cave, where engravings carved deep into the rock cover the walls of a short passage. The final phase in the sequence of Aboriginal cave art styles, shallow engravings, found in caves such as Malangine and Koongine, is characterized by 'shallow incisions usually executed with single strokes of a pointed tool'.[11]

Other notable archaeological cave sites in Australia are found in karst areas in the inland southwestern part of Tasmania. Some of these were occupied continuously for as long as 20,000 years, while others appear only to have provided temporary shelter to hunting parties. Two cave sites are of particular interest. The Ballawinne cave in the Maxwell River Valley contains a stencil gallery with 23 outlines of hands in the cave's dark zone, some of which are 'stunning in their clarity – vivid red ochre against the scalloped pale grey dolomite wall',[12] believed to date back roughly 14,000 years, as well as red ochre markings on the walls, ceilings, floor and on five protuberances, proving that Aboriginal peoples in Tasmania practised stencilling and

rock painting in the Ice Age. Another twenty-plus stencils and extensive red ochre smears have been found in Tasmania's Wargata Mina (Judds Cavern), one of the longest river caves in Australia, located deep in rainforest in the Cracroft Valley. The stencils are in a chamber the size of a suburban house, obscured by a curtain of stalactites, and executed with a red pigment that contains traces of human blood.[13]

Joseph Wright of Derby, *A Cavern, Evening*, 1774, oil on canvas.

If art produced *in* caves has been largely the preserve of archaeologists and scientists (now more than ever as caves are increasingly locked or kept secret to protect the fragile art inside), art *depicting* caves has for centuries enjoyed widespread appeal and is testament to our fascination with the earth's hollow places.

On 13 August 1772 the scientist Joseph Banks (of *Endeavour* fame), visiting the Scottish island of Staffa in the company of a

Dr Solander and a Dr Lind, came upon a cave 'which the natives call *the cave of Fingal*; its length is 371 feet [113.1 m], its height about 115 feet [35 m], and its width 51 feet [15.5 m]; the whole side is solid rock, and the bottom is covered with water 12 feet [3.7 m] deep'.[14] Banks's visit heralded those of countless other luminaries, including Sir Walter Scott, John Keats, J.M.W. Turner, William Wordsworth, Jules Verne, Felix Mendelssohn and Queen Victoria (who was rowed into the cave on the royal barge in 1847). The cave's basalt columns inspired the work of numerous artists, poets and musicians who made the pilgrimage to Staffa in the nineteenth century.

William Daniell's *A Voyage Round Great Britain* (1814–25) included several paintings in or around Fingal's Cave. The 'grand pillars of basalt standing together as thick as honey combs' are the key elements of *Exterior of Fingal's Cave, Staffa*; *Entrance to Fingal's Cave, Staffa* and *In Fingal's Cave, Staffa*.[15] But the pillars in these images are highly stylized rather than realistic representations of the cave's geomorphology; the column's rough surfaces are too smooth and the uneven broken columns too splendidly regular. Daniell's images translate 'geo-space' into a human register. This is especially clear in *Entrance to Fingal's Cave, Staffa* in which the cliff tops and surface turf appear like a massive thatched roof; and the two human figures to the right of the cave entrance (impossibly large in terms of perspective) seem visually synonymous with the columns.

Turner travelled to Staffa in stormy weather in 1830. His 'Staffa Sketch Book', with many interior views of the cave, shows that he was among those who were able to explore the cave, despite the inclement weather. One of his drawings was used to develop 'Fingal's Cave, Staffa', an illustration that appeared on the title page of the tenth volume of Scott's *Poetical Works* (1833–4). His visit also produced one of his most famous works, the painting *Staffa, Fingal's Cave*, which was exhibited at the Royal Academy in 1832. In this painting we see Turner's 'grand vision of the landscape of the cave's exterior, of Staffa's cliffs, of its sea and sky'.[16] The cave itself is indistinct,

barely visible through the rain cloud which dominates the picture, competing for the viewer's attention with the smoke issuing from the funnel of the valiant steamboat. Michael Shortland argues persuasively that even though he sketched on-site Turner's images nevertheless present a 'contrivance',

A modern impression of an aquatint, *In Fingal's Cave, Staffa*, for William Daniell's *A Voyage Round Great Britain undertaken in the summer of the year 1813* (London, 1814–25).

> with all the important elements of the image modeled, one might say, from nature and yet against nature. For one thing, the sea actually prevents access to the right side of the cave. For another, the columns are not curved but neatly perpendicular. And finally, the setting sun cannot be seen from within the cave, which faces south.[17]

Beyond visual art, the cave on Staffa has galvanized artists from across disciplines and traditions, including Wordsworth, who produced several rather undistinguished sonnets inspired by his experience of the island, and Mendelssohn, whose overture *The Hebrides*, Opus 26 (first performed 14 May 1832 at London's

Covent Garden Theatre), popularly known as the *Fingal's Cave* overture, was inspired by his visit to the cave in 1829.

A sea cave is also the subject of Sir Edward John Poynter's *The Cave of the Storm Nymphs* (probably inspired by the cave of the nymphs in Book 13 of the *Odyssey*), first exhibited at the Royal Academy in 1903. Poynter's canvas depicts three nymphs in their cave, while outside a ship caught in the storm, probably of their making, flounders. The sensual figures of the three nymphs are shown in varying states of ecstasy as the ship's treasure floats into their domain. The evident eroticism of the work spills into the space of the cave itself; the viewer is positioned to dwell on the beauty and sensuality within the cave, and to forget the wreckage beyond its mouth.

Throughout the history of art, from the half-woman, half-bison figure curved round a stalactite in the Chauvet cave to Ryan McGinley's contemporary photographs of nude women draped over or seemingly merged with speleothems, caves have

J.M.W. Turner, *Staffa, Fingal's Cave*, 1832, oil on canvas.

been linked with the female form. Henry Moore's *Four Reclining Figures: Caves* (1974) shows four abstract nude female figures reclining in different poses, each in a separate cavity against or surrounded by a green backdrop. The figures in their womb-like chambers are seductive, but the painting is primarily an image of security, the caves providing safe shelter from whatever is beyond their walls. The American artist Louisa Chase explicitly depicts the sexuality of underground openings in *Pink Cave* (1983). In her painting the cave is unequivocally a vagina, the primal opening, the passage out of which all life is born, and the anatomical composition of the work emphasizes this. Chase's pink cave, which suggests warmth, is a place to be entered, the passage to the fertile womb of mother earth, the mysterious source of all things – and as in Moore's painting, a place of shelter and security. Importantly, both paintings (especially Moore's) exploit caves as visual metaphors and recall the pictorial traditions of early rock art.

Sidney Nolan's painting *In the Cave* (1957), from his second series of 'Mrs Fraser' paintings, specifically borrows the form of an Aboriginal rock art x-ray image to depict a naked Eliza Fraser, who was shipwrecked on the Queensland coast in 1836, and held captive by local Aborigines. In Nolan's painting, Bracewell, her convict saviour, emerges in uniform from the depth of the cave behind her. More whimsically, the street artist Banksy has saluted the work of prehistoric cave painters in the fake rock art he surreptitiously hung in the British Museum in 2005, which featured a human figure hunting a wildebeest and pushing a shopping trolley (now in the museum's permanent collection), and in the 'cave painting' he produced in London's Leake Street three years later, which depicts prehistoric cave art similar to that found in caves such as Altamira or Lascaux being removed by a cleaner. In this mural he draws an immediate and obvious connection between his public art and primitive cave art traditions, as does Nolan, albeit to different effect. The cleaner is removing Banksy's art just as, given the chance, he would remove the work of the cave artists; there was a time when

Sir Edward John Poynter, *The Cave of the Storm Nymphs*, 1903, oil on canvas.

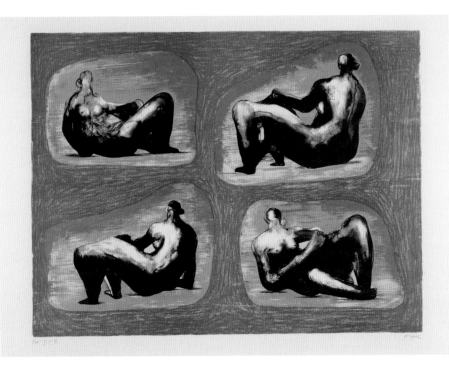

early cave art was not appreciated or protected, but now the British Museum collects the work of a 'quality vandal'.[18]

These last few works are all examples of art that has utilized the mythological and metaphorical associations of caves. Similarly, in his late nineteenth-century hanging scroll, *Meditation in a Cave*, the Chinese artist Ren Yu draws on the religious or sacred associations of caves. There is also a strong European tradition of landscape painting dating over several centuries that seeks to present caves in a largely realistic mode. A good example of this type of art is Hubert Robert's *The Mouth of a Cave* (1784), which takes its perspective from within the cave. The light in the painting focuses the viewer's eye on the threshold of the cave and the figures meeting there, the imagined hollow nothingness of the interior mirrored in the seemingly endless sea and sky beyond. In contrast *Grotto of Sarrazine near Nans-sous-Sainte-Anne* (c. 1864), by the French realist painter Gustave Courbet, focuses entirely on the cave itself, on the form and

Henry Moore, *Four Reclining Figures: Cave*, 1974, lithograph on paper.

colour of the rock. While there are no human figures to distract the viewer, the very rock appears alive. While Courbet both draws us to contemplate the mouth of the cave and blocks our entry, Patrick Caulfield transports us into the belly in *View Inside a Cave* (1965). Already inside the cave, the viewer of Caulfield's two-tone grey work (which recalls the aesthetics of the comic book) is lured further into the expansive, strikingly inorganic darkness, rather than enticed out of it. The emphasis on geology, evident in the works of both Courbet and Caulfield, is a hallmark of much present-day cave art.

The underground landscape has also inspired many cavers to take up brush or pencil, or to work clay or wood. Notable among these caver artists, whose work is intended to appeal to a caving subculture rather than to have resonance with a broader

Louisa Chase, *Pink Cave*, 1983, oil on canvas.

artistic culture, are Robin Gray and Rhian Hicks. Gray's work is characterized by the close attention he pays to both the form of the cave and to the equipment of the caver. Hicks's work, including her watercolour *The Bridge*, consistently captures the beauty and fragility of her underground subjects. In the United States caving has influenced Michael Kehl's work in wood, including his decorative vessels.

The work of members of the International Society for Spelaeological Art (ISSA) or the SpeleoArt group reminds us that before the advent of photography, artists followed the explorers, sketching or painting their underground discoveries. However, since Alfred Brothers successfully photographed a chamber in the Blue John Caverns in Derbyshire in 1865,[19] photography has increasingly become the favoured medium for

Sidney Nolan, *In the Cave*, 1957, polyvinyl acetate paint on hardboard.

John Stezaker, *Mask XXXV*, 2007, collage.

documenting caves. Today, with the development of digital photography and lighting techniques, photography has become perhaps the most practised art form underground. Chris Howes has been photographing caves since 1968, first with film stock and now with digital equipment. His photograph of a caver in Ogof Ffynnon Ddu focuses on human interaction with the underground, capturing the movement of both caver and cave. Pioneering underwater cave photographers Wes Skiles and Jill Heinerth have taken the art of underwater photography and cinematography to levels that few could have imagined even as recently as the beginning of this century. Their art defines and augments the space of the underwater caverns and the fragile

architecture of the caves, the speleothems formed in rock over millennia and now hidden in some of the earth's most secret places, through the camera's viewfinder.

Banksy, graffiti painted in Leake Street, London, May 2008.

The British artist John Stezaker employs postcards of caves in some of his enigmatic photographic collages. In these 'unsettling assemblages',[20] the postcards become 'masks' on the faces of stars and starlets of the 1930s and 1940s, which seem to open windows onto the human unconscious. In *Mask XXXV* a tinted postcard of Lydstep Cavern, near Tenby, obscures the face of an unidentified starlet captured in a black and white publicity shot. Rather than masking the actress's identity, the placement of the image of the cave suggests the universality of the metaphorics explored here, and in much cave art, as well as in literature.

7 'Caverns measureless to man': Caves in Literature

References to caves in literature abound. In Homer's *Odyssey*, Odysseus and twelve of his men are imprisoned in the cave of the giant Cyclops Polyphemus; in Spenser's *Faerie Queene* (1590–96) Sir Guyon visits the Cave of Mammon, the treasure-house of the god of wealth, and virtuously rejects the tempting horde of gold he finds there; and in Samuel Taylor Coleridge's great poem 'Kubla Khan' (1816), 'Where Alph, the sacred river, ran / Through caverns measureless to man', the enchanted reader discovers 'a miracle of rare device, / A sunny pleasure-dome with caves of ice!'[1] Caves feature in many of Shakespeare's plays: Timon resides in a cave in *Timon of Athens*; Imogen finds refuge in a Welsh cave in *Cymbeline*; and Prospero makes his island home in a cave in *The Tempest*. The eponymous hero of Mark Twain's *The Adventures of Tom Sawyer* (1876) is lost in a dripstone cave with Becky Thatcher; Pixy's Cave is the key to the murder in Agatha Christie's *Evil Under the Sun* (1941); and in Michael Ondaatje's *The English Patient* (1992), a badly injured Katherine Clifton dies inside the Cave of Swimmers when her lover Almásy fails to return with medical assistance. In Mary Shelley's *Frankenstein* (1818) the tortured monster finds refuge in ice caves remote from human habitation; the man-cub Mowgli is adopted and brought up by the Wolf family in their cave lair in Rudyard Kipling's *The Jungle Book* (1894); and in Patrick Süskind's *Perfume* (1985) his anti-hero, Jean-Baptiste Grenouille, spends seven years living in a cave in the Auvergne. Caves are the destination of the journeys in H. Rider

Haggard's imperial adventure novels *King Solomon's Mines* (1885) and *She* (1887); the Marabar Caves are at the centre of the mystery and muddle of E. M. Forster's *A Passage to India* (1924); and a cluster of arid caves is at the heart of Jim Crace's *Quarantine* (1997).

While, as we have seen, the science of speleology has drawn on the vocabulary of the earth's surface – of the human body and architecture – to describe the underground world of caves, lit-

Illustrations by Peter Hay with lettering by Pip Hall for Samuel Taylor Coleridge's poem 'Kubla Khan' (2004 edition).

In Xanadu did Kubla Khan A stately pleasure-dome decree:

Where Alph, the sacred river, ran

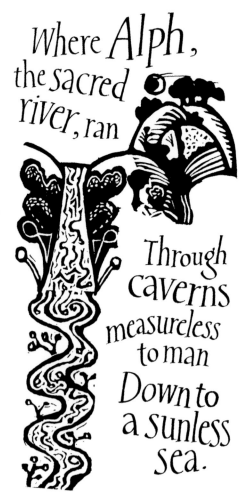

Through caverns measureless to man Down to a sunless sea.

erature has in turn drawn on caves for imagery with which to understand the human condition on the surface. So while caves are everywhere in literature, caves are rarely what a literary text is actually about. Or to put it another way, science thinks *about* caves, while literature thinks *with* caves. Caves in literature are places of concealment or containment: they are used as symbols of the womb and the tomb; they are places of nefarious activity, and sources of wealth; they are doors to the underworld, and mirrors of the soul; they are repositories of secrets, and keys to truth. They are places people enter and leave; they are silent and many voiced; they are places of knowing and not knowing. And they are frequently sources of artistic creativity.

The myriad ways caves have been used, literally and metaphorically, in literature over more than a millennium are succinctly captured in three 'cave poems': Coleridge's 'Kubla Khan'; W. H. Auden's 'In Praise of Limestone' (1951); and Robert Penn Warren's 'Speleology' (1979).

The 'caverns measureless to man' encountered in Coleridge's 'Kubla Khan' are among the best known caves in English literature. The poem is evoked in diverse texts from Barbara Hurd's *Entering the Stone: On Caves and Feeling through the Dark* to James Cameron's 3D film *Sanctum* (2011). In Cameron's film the curmudgeonly veteran cave diver Frank McGuire (Richard Roxburgh) recites the poem to himself and later to his son in moments of awe or desperation; it is something he passes on to his son before his death, a gift in turn from the young man's absent mother. For the cinema audience the poem accompanies moments of claustrophobia; it is simultaneously comfortingly familiar and unknown, a fleeting moment in the twilight between the outside world and the cave. For McGuire and now in turn for his son, the poem penetrates the majesty of caves without revealing their mystery, and serves as an explanation of McGuire's life. Indeed, 'Kubla Khan' appears to be the go-to poem for the makers of cave adventure or horror films, including both *Sanctum* and Bruce Hunt's *The Cave* (2005). Coleridge's poem also provides the title for David Poyer's Tiller Galloway cave-diving thriller, *Down to a Sunless*

Scoff Schofield in
Joint Hole in the
Yorkshire Dales.

Sea (1996), set in the acquifers of North Florida, and the title
and epigraph of Sheck Exley's cave-diving memoir, *Caverns
Measureless to Man* (1994).

Coleridge's poem begins with a description of Kubla Khan's
Xanadu, situated near the river Alph, which flows through
caverns before reaching an underground sea:

In Xanadu did Kubla Khan
A stately pleasure-dome decree:
Where Alph, the sacred river, ran
Through caverns measureless to man
Down to a sunless sea.[2]

Xanadu is presented as a man-made garden paradise, enclosed, like Eden, by walls. It is contrasted with the infinite, 'savage' beauty of the natural caves, the 'caverns measureless to man' and the 'caves of ice'. It is from this subterranean darkness that the fountain erupts, suggesting that true creativity comes from within, from the dark places of the earth or the soul.

In this seminal poem Coleridge defines caves in relation to man. If a cave is a hole large enough for a human to enter, here the caverns are measureless, suggesting something infinite, beyond the ken of humankind. The cave in Coleridge's poem is beyond human comprehension, almost impossible to describe or talk about. There is a sense in this poem that if we are to understand these underground spaces, we must do so on a spiritual level, through our senses, hearing 'the mingled measure [tune] / From the fountain and the caves'.[3]

W. H. Auden, who numbers among the greatest poets of the twentieth century, invokes the spirit of Coleridge's 'Kubla Khan' in the 'gesticulating fountains, / Made solely for pleasure' he describes in his much anthologized poem 'In Praise of Limestone'. Auden's poem begins with the lines:

If it form the one landscape that we, the inconstant ones,
Are consistently homesick for, this is chiefly
Because it dissolves in water. Mark these rounded slopes
With their surface fragrance of thyme and, beneath,
A secret system of caves and conduits;[4]

It is evident even in this short extract that Auden uses the inconsistency of karst geology to explore the contingencies of the human condition. Robert Macfarlane eulogizes Auden's love of limestone:

Cover design for the first UK edition of Robert Penn Warren's *The Cave* (1959).

W. H. Auden, who so loved the karst shires of the Northern Pennines, adored limestone. What most moved him about it was the way it eroded. Limestone's solubility in water means that any fault-lines in the original rock get slowly deepened by a process of soft liquid wear. In this way, the form into which limestone grows over time is determined by its first flaws. For Auden, this was a human as well as a

geological quality: he found in limestone an honesty –
an acknowledgement that we are as defined by our faults
as by our substance.[5]

As a sedimentary rock, limestone is simultaneously durable and
impermanent, shaped by the water that both creates its forms
and destroys them. The geology Auden evokes in the poem is
thus a metaphor for immortality and mortality, for the strengths
and the weaknesses of humans. Limestone, like humans, is stable
only to a point; both, Auden suggests, are ultimately shaped or
determined by forces beyond their control.

There is a marked increase in the use of geological language
in Auden's poem compared to Coleridge's, which is in keeping
with the development of cave science between 1797, when
Coleridge composed 'Kubla Khan', and 1948, when Auden wrote
his poem. There is also a concomitant anthropomorphizing of the
caves in Auden's poem. Whereas Coleridge gestures in this direction, there are voices throughout Auden's verse, chuckling, crying,
purring, whispering and murmuring from the secret caves and
underground streams beneath the limestone landscape.

The language of cave science is promoted to the title of the
American poet Robert Penn Warren's autobiographical poem
'Speleology', which captures well the atmosphere of caves and the
thrill of exploration. Similarly, the anthropomorphizing of caves
in Auden's poem is taken a step further in Warren's when the cave
and the narrator are conflated as the boy feels his 'Heart beating
as though to a pulse of darkness and earth'.[6] And the voices that
emerged from the caves in Coleridge's and Auden's poems continue to be heard in Warren's, as if to demonstrate Gaston
Bachelard's aphorism: 'All caves speak' ('*Toutes les grottes parlent*').[7]

While Warren's cave may be a real place – he grew up in the
Kentucky karst region – the poem also neatly explores the symbolic possibilities of the cave as both womb and tomb. At the age
of six the poem's protagonist discovers the 'cave-mouth / Under
ledges moss-green, and moss-green the inner dark'. On each suc-
cessive visit he 'peered in, crept further', until at the age of twelve,
armed with a flashlight, he pushes far enough into the cavern to

discover 'Where chambers of darkness rose and stalactites down-stabbed', 'To see the lone life there, the cave-cricket pale / As a ghost on my brown arm', and to feel 'darkness and depth and no Time'. This escape from time, presented as a dream in Coleridge's poem but more vividly real here, recurs over and over again in caves in literature. The boy's physical exploration of the cave is echoed in the psychological insights into the self, and the womb/tomb experience of 'a darkness so absolute'.[8] The cave in Warren's poem engulfs the young explorer. It is simultaneously personified as a female body that is entered, and somewhat para-doxically as a male body which thrusts and debouches. It is also the birth canal and the channel back to the womb, and negotiating the passage in either direction signals a change of state.

Symbolic representations of the cave as a womb or tomb are so numerous in literature that they are almost commonplace. In Shakespeare's *Henry V*, for example, the caves of France are likened to 'womby vaultages'.[9] Thomas Hardy employs the cave as a rather blunt image of the womb in his poem 'The Cave of the Unborn'; and in John Steinbeck's *The Grapes of Wrath* (1939) the cave in which Tom Joad hides is symbolic of the womb.

In Forster's *A Passage to India*, the main characters are defined by their reactions to the mysterious Marabar Caves. Adela Quested's hysteria, which leads to her accusation of assault against the Indian Dr Aziz, is brought on when she confronts her repressed inner self in the caves. The hollowness and roundness of the caves suggest they contain nothing, but everything is con-tained in that cosmic nothingness. As Wilfred Stone explains,

> the caves are the primal womb from which we all came and the primal tomb to which we all return; they are the darkness before existence itself. Some can contemplate that nothingness, others cannot.[10]

Caves are a key feature, too, of the topography of the island in Daniel Defoe's *Robinson Crusoe* (1719), where they provide Crusoe with both shelter and sanctuary. Indeed he feels so secure after discovering his second cave residence, his

An illustration of Crusoe's cave, for an 1820s edition of Daniel Defoe's *Robinson Crusoe*.

vaulted 'Retreat', that he 'fancy'd [him]self now like one of the ancient Giants, which are said to live in Caves and Holes in the Rocks, where none could come at them'.[11] Earlier in the novel Crusoe makes his main residence, his 'Castle', in a cave he extends behind his tent. This well-ordered space, which 'look'd like a Magazine of all Necessary things',[12] is also a place of self-discovery. Crusoe's comfortable life on the island is thrown into turmoil following his sighting of the savages at their cannibal feast. For the next year he lives in fear, unable to continue his improvements to the island in case his activities or smoke from a fire attracts the attention of visiting cannibals. His life is turned around again, however, by the discovery of a second cave, 'a hollow Place' fashioned by Nature,[13] which he explores with the aid of candles and a tinder-box. Located at the back of this cave is a small tunnel which, when crawled through, leads to a much larger, womb-like, second chamber, 'a most delightful Cavity, or Grotto', a place of rare beauty that affords him amniotic security, and which, unlike his first cave, is wholly the work of nature:

> never was such a glorious Sight seen in the Island, I dare say, as it was, to look round the Sides and Roof of this Vault, or Cave; the Walls reflected 100 thousand Lights to me from my two Candles; what it was in Rock, whether Diamonds, or any other precious Stones, or Gold, which I rather suppos'd it to be, I knew not.[14]

These passages, in what is arguably the first novel in English, clearly demonstrate that in the early eighteenth century the lexicon of caves has still not been formulated, and Defoe struggles for synonyms. In the space of less than two pages he uses the following words and phrases: cave, hollow place, holes in the rock, vault, cavity and grotto. The cave serves Crusoe both as a store for his powder magazine and spare arms, and a fortress where, in a metaphoric return to the womb, he can remain safe.

The womb symbolism buried in Forster's and Defoe's caves comes to the surface in Michel Tournier's *Friday* (*Vendredi*,

1967), a remarkable retelling of *Robinson Crusoe*. Penetrating deeper into the cave that served him as a storehouse than he had previously done, Tournier's Robinson finds the opening of a narrow vertical chimney, which, after several unsuccessful attempts to negotiate, he finally succeeds in passing through head-first after having stripped off his clothes and rubbed his body with milk. On exploring with his hands the pitch-black crypt he has entered, Robinson locates a cavity or recess into which – with 'knees drawn up to his chin, shins crossed, hands resting on his feet'[15] – he fits exactly. The physical exploration of the void is echoed by Robinson's psychological exploration of his soul, the empty space of the cave echoing the solitude of the castaway.

A good example of the use of caves as a representation of the tomb is found in Michael Ondaatje's Booker Prize-winning novel *The English Patient*, later adapted into an Academy Award-winning film by Anthony Minghella (1996). In Ondaatje's work the Cave of Swimmers, so named for the prehistoric drawings of swimming figures adorning its walls, is the most important of Almásy's discoveries in the Gilf Kebir region of the Sahara Desert, and the site of two of the most important scenes in the novel. In the first of these Almásy is forced to leave his injured lover Katherine Clifton in the cave, which is destined to become her tomb when he is prevented from returning in time to save her. In the second, when he returns to retrieve her body three years later, Almásy enters the cave naked, and there is a clear suggestion of intimacy with his dead lover's desiccated corpse. In this crucial, disturbing cave scene Ondaatje intersects the multiple images of the womb and the tomb that are so frequently associated with caves in literature.

The multi-faceted binaries of the surface and the deep present in Ondaatje's novel feature strongly in the first major poem in English, the eighth-century Anglo-Saxon epic *Beowulf*, which tells of two major events in the life of the Geatish hero Beowulf: the first when in his youth he fights the demonic Grendel and then his mother who comes to avenge her son's death; and the second, 50 years later, when he does battle with a dragon. In the poem Grendel's mother's lair is hidden in the depths of a mere in the middle of a dark swamp. This vaulted chamber is the antithesis of the bright world of Heorot, the court of the Danish king Hrothgar that Beowulf protects. Her cave is a dark, dank, hell-like place which represents evil, and Beowulf's victory over Grendel's mother is all the greater because the battle takes place in this foul lair.

In the early fourteenth century the Italian Dante Alighieri's *Inferno*, the first part of his masterpiece *The Divine Comedy*, takes the reader on a terrifying tour of Satan's domain at the centre of the earth. The belief, embedded in Dante's poem, that caves might be portals to the underworld is emphasized by E. A. Martel in his article 'Speleology, or Cave Exploration' (1899):

> In my excursions over the plateaus of the Causses I
> frequently met, at the level of the surface, open, dark-holes,
> and mouths of vertical wells – *avens* – the depths of which
> no one had ever looked into, unsoundable, they said, which
> the peasants naturally took to be the real mouths of hell.[16]

While caves are most often envisaged as doors *into* the underworld, they can also be doors through which dark creatures emerge *out of* the underworld. In J.R.R. Tolkien's *The Lord of the Rings*, the One Ring was forged in and brought out of the chasm known as the Cracks of Doom in the Chambers of Fire, a long, high-roofed cave in the cone of Mount Doom that was the heart of the wizard Sauron's evil realm, and it was from the caverns of the Misty Mountains that the cave trolls emerged. Indeed Tolkien's Middle Earth is riddled with caves, including the 'vast and beautiful' Glittering Caves, the Caverns of Helm's Deep in Rohan, which the dwarf Gimli describes as 'one of the marvels of the Northern World . . . immeasurable halls, filled with an everlasting music of water that tinkles into pools'.[17]

In sixteenth- and seventeenth-century literature caves such as 'Those grim and horrid caves, / Whose lookes affright the day' in Michael Drayton's 'An Ode Written in the Peake' (1606) are often meeting places for rogues and gypsies.[18] The wonderfully named Devil's Arse (Peak Cavern) in the

Derbyshire Peak District, which, according to William Camden who succinctly captures the two principal tropes for representing caves – buildings and bodily orifices – 'gapeth with a wide mouth, and hath in it many turnings and retyring roomes', is a gathering place where 'th'AEgiptians throng in clusters' each year in Ben Jonson's masque *The Gypsies Metamorphosed* (1621).[19] As Bachelard explains, the cave is one of the three great images of refuge, which function in literature as an avenue

'To those who enter the hall of the dead, evil comes', illustration by Walter Paget for H. Rider Haggard's *King Solomon's Mines* (1888 edition).

of return to the mother.[20] The cave as an image of refuge is evident again in Ernest Hemingway's *For Whom the Bell Tolls* (1940), where caves provide a strategic hiding place for a group of loyalist guerrillas planning to blow up a bridge behind enemy lines as part of an offensive against Franco's Fascists during the Spanish Civil War.

As cave exploration took off in the nineteenth century, there was an increasing use of caves as physical settings in literature, particularly in adventure fiction. Caves are prominent features in H. Rider Haggard's exemplary Victorian adventure novels, *King Solomon's Mines* and *She*: in *She*, the home of Ayesha is a series of cavernous tombs deep beneath a dormant volcano; in *King Solomon's Mines*, often regarded as the founding fiction of the lost world genre, the frozen corpse of the Portuguese explorer José Silvestra is found seated in a cave, while the mines of the title are a vast treasure house carved deep into a mountain in Haggard's fictional Kukuanaland.

It is a short step from exploring under volcanoes to considering the idea of a hollow earth, of a planet that is either hollow or contains a huge interior space or series of spaces. This idea, endorsed by John Cleves Symmes Jr and others, but long dismissed by scientists, is a key feature of subterranean fiction, which as its name suggests, is characterized by its underground settings. Edgar Allan Poe draws on the hollow earth theory in his novel *The Narrative of Arthur Gordon Pym of Nantucket* (1838), and Edward Bulwer-Lytton's early science fiction novel, *The Coming Race* (1871), is about the discovery of a subterranean world occupied by the descendants of an antediluvian civilization. Lewis Carroll's *Alice's Adventures in Wonderland* (1865) is set in the underground world that Alice discovers after she accidentally falls down a rabbit hole, while the title characters have to find their way back from the centre of the earth in *Dorothy and the Wizard in Oz* (1908), one of L. Frank Baum's many sequels to *The Wonderful Wizard of Oz* (1900). Edgar Rice Burroughs set all seven novels of his Pellucidar adventure series, beginning with *At the Earth's Core* (1914) and including one Tarzan story, in a hollow earth.

By far the most famous example of this subgenre of adventure fiction, however, is Jules Verne's classic *Journey to the Centre of the Earth* (1864). This novel, packed with scientific information, follows the journey of the German Professor Lidenbrock, his nephew Axel and their Icelandic guide Hans through volcanic tubes to an underground sea in 'a sort of grotto, of considerable size',[21] 87 miles under the surface of the earth. Their journey into the hollow core is another symbolic journey into the self, and the human condition more generally. It also shows that 150 years after Defoe, writers were still struggling to find words to describe the subterranean world. As Axel observes in the underground cavern that marks the furthest point in their journey:

> The word 'cavern' is clearly insufficient for my attempt to convey this immense place. The words which make up human language are inadequate for those who venture into the depths of the Earth.[22]

The nineteenth-century fascination with underground adventure popularized by Verne and others shows no sign of abating. Recent additions to the genre include Clive Cussler's twelfth Dirk Pitt novel, *Inca Gold* (1994), a classic treasure hunt along an unexplored underground river, and Jeff Long's *The Descent* (1999), a contemporary hollow earth novel.

Caves have also proved a popular location for mystery stories over many decades. The two-million-year-old Kents Cavern in Torquay, Devon, is accurately depicted as Hampsly Cavern in Agatha Christie's mystery *The Man in the Brown Suit* (1924), in which Colonel Race makes his first appearance. In her novel *The Sittaford Mystery* (1931) Pixy's Cave was to be the escaped prisoner's hideout, and the same cave also features in the Hercule Poirot mystery *Evil Under the Sun* (1941). The Lechuguilla Caves in New Mexico are the setting for Nevada Barr's Anna Pigeon mystery *Blind Descent*, in which her park ranger heroine battles her own claustrophobia to find out what happened to her caver friend badly injured in a

'The Guiding Stream',
illustration by Édouard
Riou for Jules Verne's
*Journey to the Centre of
the Earth* (1864).

suspicious accident underground. In each of these works, as in others like them, the enclosed underground setting heightens the tension of the mystery.

Caves also feature prominently in several important adventure fictions and mysteries for children and young adults. By far the most famous cave episode in American literature is found in Mark Twain's *The Adventures of Tom Sawyer*. In

Twain's novel Tom and Becky Thatcher are lost in the maze of
McDougal's Cave, 'a vast labyrinth of crooked aisles that ran
into each other and out again and led nowhere',[23] where Tom
and his friends later find Murrel's hidden gold. Tom and Becky
survive their three-day ordeal underground when Tom chances
on a way out, after a series of incidents that bear striking simi-
larities to some of Axel's experiences in Verne's novel.[24] As
Twain warns his readers (and cavers), 'No man "knew" the
cave. That was an impossible thing.'[25] (After the publication
of Twain's novel, the cave on which he based McDougal's Cave
became the first show cave in Missouri and was later renamed
Mark Twain Cave.)

In Enid Blyton's *Secret Seven Win Through* (1955) the
Secret Seven choose a cave as their temporary meeting place
while their shed is being cleaned and painted. In *The Valley of
Adventure* (1947), the third book of Blyton's Adventure Series,
Jack, Philip, Dinah and Lucy-Ann find themselves caught up

Cave diagram from the
endpapers of the first
edition of Nevada Barr's
Blind Descent (1998).

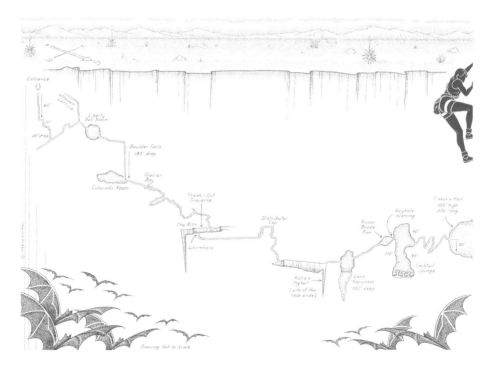

Cover design for Richard Church's *The Cave* (1950).

in an adventure in a deserted valley. As the tale unfolds the children explore a series of tunnels and caves, including the Cave of Echoes, the Cave of Stalactites and the Cave of Stars. In a similar vein, *The Secret of the Caves* (1929), the seventh volume of the original Hardy Boys series by Franklin W. Dixon, takes the young detectives to the Honeycomb Caves, where, after a series of dangerous encounters, they solve the mystery. The abundance of caves in children's literature, where they are an easy device for the setting of mysteries and adventures, also signals their imaginative function as retreats from the normative world of adults.

Richard Church takes his young readers in a different direction in *The Cave* (1950). This novel, which is something of a subterranean meeting of Enid Blyton's Famous Five adventures and William Golding's *Lord of the Flies* (1954), depicts boys becoming men while underground. While lost in the cave the boys begin to understand the nuances of John's father's claim that 'exploring caves' is 'the foundation of our knowledge of the human race'.[26]

For more than a millennium, authors of poetry, fiction and drama have used caves to explore the human condition. To this end, the subterranean landscape is frequently personified, as it is in two extraordinary American stories.

In H. P. Lovecraft's 'The Beast in the Cave', a man touring Mammoth Cave becomes lost after he is separated from his guide. After his torch expires he begins to give up hope of finding a way out of the pitch dark, when he hears footsteps approaching him. Afraid that the footsteps might belong to a lost mountain lion or other animal, he fells the approaching beast with a stone. The guide returns to find the lost tourist, and together they examine the fallen creature and discover that it is a pale, deformed human, who had also become lost in the cave.

The disorientating underground setting proves to be a great leveller in Stephen Crane's beautifully crafted sketch 'Four Men in a Cave' (1892), which recounts the tall tale of four hunters who set out to explore a cave and soon become afraid in the unfamiliar environment:

Things that hung seemed to be on the wet, uneven ceiling, ready to drop upon the men's bare necks. Under their hands the clammy floor seemed alive and writhing. When the little man endeavored to stand erect the ceiling forced him down. Knobs and points came out and punched him.[27]

In this story the personification of the cave is such that it resists the intruders, pushing, punching and hitting the four men who, driven by their fear, quarrel, fall and find themselves lying 'in a heap upon the floor of a gray chamber' where in a moment of terror they come face-to-face with a grey-bearded hermit and their own pomposity.[28]

The hermit in Crane's tale highlights the domestic use of caves, which is another common trope in literature. In Rudyard Kipling's *Just So Stories* (1902) Woman picks out a dry cave as a home for Man and herself, where they raise a family and domesticate animals such as the Cat, Dog and Horse. In a similar vein, Mervyn Peake's powerful play *The Cave*, written in the mid-1950s, is a three-act drama set in a cave over three distinct time periods: the Neolithic period, the Middle Ages and the Modern period. The cave in Peake's work functions as a microcosmic setting where thousands of years of human history are played out, and human time is juxtaposed with geological time to great effect.

Works *about* caves and references *to* caves may abound in literature, but there is no evidence to suggest that writers have actually produced their work *in* caves. Evelyn Waugh came close: he corrected the proofs of *Brideshead Revisited* (1945) while hiding in a cave during active service in Yugoslavia during the Second World War.[29]

Martin Baines in a showerbath, Dow Cave, Yorkshire.

Gustave Doré, *The Burial of Sarah*, 1866, engraving.

8 Sacred Symbols: Holy Caves

Caves have played a prominent role in the sacred life of all the world's major religions and spiritual traditions, including the Abrahamic religions (Judaism, Christianity, Islam), the Indian religions (Hinduism, Jainism, Buddhism) and the East Asian religions (Taoism, Confucianism). According to Christian tradition, Jesus was entombed in a burial cave belonging to Joseph of Arimathea prior to his resurrection. The Indian Buddhist monk Bodhidharma, the patriarch of Ch'an or Zen Buddhism, was interred in a cave following his death on the banks of the Luo River. From ancient times they have been used as burial sites and as places of worship. The Cave of the Patriarchs, also known as the Cave of Machpelah (the cave of the double tombs), demonstrates this dual function. This subterranean system is located in the old city of Hebron on the West Bank below a massive shrine complex built by Herod the Great during the first century BCE. It is sacred to all three Abrahamic religions. After the Temple on the Mount in Jerusalem, it is the second holiest site for Jews, who believe it is the burial site of the Hebrew patriarchs and their wives: Abraham and Sarah; Isaac and Rebekah; and Jacob and Leah. It is also a sacred site for Muslims and Christians, both of whom venerate Abraham as a prophet of their respective gods. According to the Book of Genesis, 'Abraham buried his wife Sarah in the cave of the field of Machpelah before Mamre: the same is Hebron in the land of Canaan', and 'his sons Isaac and Ishmael buried him in the cave of Machpelah, in the field of Ephron the son of Zohar the

Hittite, which is before Mamre' with Sarah.[1] The burials of Isaac, Rebekah, Leah and Jacob in the cave of Machpelah are recorded in later chapters.[2] The Cave of the Patriarchs is, then, first a burial site, holy because of its association with the dead; the shrine complex serves to mark the holy place below, the Cave of Machpelah.

This dual pattern is common to many holy cave sites around the world, regardless of the religion that holds them sacred. First, there is an association with a divinity or holy person, living or dead. Holy caves may be burial sites, or they may be shelters where a hermit or fakir, anchorite or monk took up residence. In the Judaeo-Christian tradition caves are identified with the early monastic traditions. They have commonly been depicted as places of exile or refuge, where Christian hermits could escape both persecution by the Roman authorities and the temptations of the world. Monks belonging to Indian and Asian religions have for thousands of years meditated in caves. The sepulchral caves of the holy commonly became sites of devotion, which in turn were marked by the construction of a place of worship of some kind, a temple, a church or a mosque. Similarly caves which sheltered holy men have frequently been extended, internally or externally, to become hermitages or monasteries. Over millennia, karst formations around the world have been claimed and tamed in the name of the sacred. Religious monuments and shrines have been cut out of cliffs; rock shelters have been expanded into cave temples; and churches have been built in the cathedral-like chambers of larger cave entrances. Sometimes these sacred caves are small, personal shrines. The entrance to Deeti's shrine in *River of Smoke* (2011), the second volume of Amitav Ghosh's *Ibis* trilogy, 'is no more than a tilted fissure in the cliffside, so narrow that it seemed impossible that a cavern could lie hidden behind it.' Yet on family outings, having followed Deeti through the fissure, the children would 'run to the part of the shrine that Deeti called her "puja-room": a small hollow in the rock, hidden away at the back', or 'stare in wonder at the painted walls of the cavern that was known as Deetiji's "Memory-Temple" – *Deetiji-ka-smitri-mandir*'.[3]

Many of the caves that have been utilized for sacred purposes over the centuries are rock shelters or small caves without deep interiors; as George Crothers, P. Willey and Patty Jo Watson remind us, 'no ancient people ever actually inhabited cave dark zones', though they did use them 'as storage locales, depositories for the dead or places to contact the spirit world'.[4] From Europe to Asia holy men and women have chosen the entrances of caves for shelter, laying claim to the twilight zones, not through any interest in the caves for themselves, but as part of a continuum of sacred use, from burial to refuge, to development as sites of pilgrimage and tourism.

Over time and space, caves have provided shelter or refuge to holy persons from across the world's religions. According to legend, St Paul of Thebes, commonly regarded as the first Christian hermit or anchorite, fled to the Theban desert as a young man to avoid persecution and made his home in a cave where he would remain for the rest of his life, sustained by water from a nearby spring and fruit from a palm tree. Similarly St Anthony the Great, widely considered the founder of Christian monasticism, lived as a hermit in a small natural cave in the mountains that follow the coast of the Red Sea. In Scotland a small littoral cave (a sea cave formed by wave action) was used as a shelter by St Ninian, the missionary who built the first Christian church in Scotland in 397 CE. There is evidence that the cave has been visited by pilgrims since the early Middle Ages, and many religious symbols have been carved into the rock both inside and outside the cave. St Ninian's Cave was used as a location in the 1973 cult film *The Wicker Man* (though the scenes inside the cave were not filmed in St Ninian's cave, but in a larger cave elsewhere).

In the sixth century CE the Buddhist Bodhidharma spent nine years in deep meditation in a mountain cave near Shao Lin Temple in Lo-yang, China. In the early seventh century CE the Muslim prophet Muhammad received his first revelation from Allah through the archangel Jibreel (Gabriel) while he was meditating in the cave of Hira, a small cave on the Jabal al-Nur mountain, near Mecca. The Sof Omar Caves in Ethiopia provided refuge to a Muslim holy man in the twelfth century CE,

Sir Herbert Maxwell, 'St. Ninian's Cave, Glasserton, Wigtownshire, Scotland, after excavations', 1885, pencil drawing which appeared as a lithograph.

and continue to be 'revered as sacred shrines'.[5] These caves have been extensively explored since Arthur Donaldson-Smith's visit in 1897. In 1967 a team led by Eric Robson successfully 'penetrate[d] the cave from end to end',[6] and in 1972 the British Speleological Expedition to Ethiopia, which drew on members of various caving clubs including two from the Preston Cave Club, surveyed the full length of the system, which at 15.1 km is the longest in Ethiopia. The cave contains many significant geological formations, such as a unique series of interconnected phreatic arches known as the Chamber of Columns.[7]

And caves continue to draw holy men and women in search of seclusion. In 1976 the English-born Buddhist nun, Tenzin Palmo, entered a remote 'cave in the snow' in Lahaul 4,000 m up in the Indian Himalayas, where she spent the next twelve years alone, growing her own food, meditating, speaking to no one, in search of enlightenment as a woman. For Tenzin Palmo, as for her predecessors, 'the cave remained the hothouse for Enlightenment'.[8]

Caves, however, have not only been places of shelter or refuge for religious hermits. Around the globe caves have been claimed for religious rites. Cave temples have been constructed in the entrances and twilight zones of caves; once isolated caves have been transformed into sites of mass worship and pilgrimage and, more recently, tourism.

The Armanath Cave temple, located 3,888 m above sea level in the Indian Himalayas, has been an object of pilgrimage for Hindus since at least the third century CE. This natural karst rock shelter is considered holy because of the dramatic ice stalagmite formations it houses, the largest of which is worshipped as an ice lingam, the phallic symbol of Shiva. Two smaller ice pillars are believed to represent Shiva's wife, Parvati, and his son, the elephant-headed Ganesh. Each year in July and August the cave is visited by up to half a million devotees of Shiva (who, ironically, threaten the very existence of the lingam they come to worship as their presence in the cave slowly causes it to melt).

In Asia many of the extraordinary architectural structures loosely referred to as 'cave temples' are not located in true caves at all, but are rock-hewn temples, fashioned by humans out of more or less vertical cliffs and other rock formations, sometimes incorporating or extending an existing natural cave. In India the Ellora Caves near Aurangabad in Maharashtra, which extend over 2 km and are dedicated to Buddhism, Hinduism and Jainism, were carved out of the wall of a basalt cliff as acts of devotion between 600 and 1000 CE; the Varaha Cave temple in Mamallapuram in Tamil Nadu, a mandapa (rock-cut sanctuary) with bas-reliefs representing the acts of Varaha, one of the ten principal avatars of Vishnu, is a good example of Pallava rock-cut architecture from the seventh century CE; while the Elephanta Caves on Gharapuri Island off the coast of Bombay are a collection of rock-cut caves dedicated to Shiva. The largest and best-preserved cave-temple complex in Sri Lanka is the Dambulla cave temple, where prehistoric rock-shelter residences were transformed into shrines over the course of a millennium. The caves, which were excavated into the rock and screened by brick walls built across the entrances, contain statues of the Buddha carved out of the rock, and religious and secular wall paintings. In China the Magao Caves, the best-known of the Dunhuang Caves in Gansu province on the old Silk Route, were constructed between the fourth and fourteenth centuries, and are famous for their remarkable collection of Buddhist murals; the Yungang Grottoes in Shanxi province are an outstanding example of Chinese Buddhist rock-cut architecture constructed in the late fifth and early sixth centuries; and the Buddhist Longmen Caves cut into the hillside above the Yi River in Henan Province include some 1,350 caves carved out of the karst cliffs over a 500-year period from 492 CE.

In Europe cave temples were more often developed in natural caves. Sveta jama (Holy Cave), located on a hill below Castle Socerb, is the only subterranean church in Slovenia. Masses are still held there every week, and there is an annual festival held in honour of Saint Socerb (Servulus), who is said to have lived in the cave before his execution in 284 CE. Today there is a steady flow of both pilgrims and tourists to the cave. Unusually for a religious site, Sveta jama is managed by the local caving club, Jamarsko društvo Dimnice Koper, which in 2007 installed mobile LED lighting in the cave that had previously been lit only by carbide lamps and electric torches.[9] Though small and barely developed, the cave has a history of religious worship dating back

A reclining Buddha in the entrance chamber of Saddan cave, Burma.

at least 400 years, and was described in some detail by the seventeenth-century polymath Johann Weichard von Valvasor.

In Italy's Natisone Valley the extensive cave system found in a limestone thrust sheet near the village of Antro is of significant speleological and historical interest, as well as housing an important religious site dating back to the early Christian period. Today the cave church of San Giovanni d'Antro, which was completely restored in the fifteenth century, clings to a mountainside in the Julian Alps, partly constructed externally, and partly built into the cave. Inside, visitors can worship, admire the religious art or venture a few hundred metres further along a rough path winding past rimstone pools and limestone concretions. The system has not yet been fully explored, though speleologists have now surveyed about 5 km of passages.

In Budapest the Christian hermit Saint Istvan (Ivan) made his home in a cave on Gellért Hill during the Middle Ages, curing the sick with thermal water from the spring in front of his cave. In 1926 the original cave, which consisted of an entrance room and connecting niches, was expanded by Pauline monks to establish a grotto chapel which copied that at Lourdes. Closed by the Communists in 1951, the church, with its natural rock walls, was reopened in 1989, and today serves as both a chapel and a heritage tourism site. While the hill owes its present name to Bishop Gellért, the patron saint of Budapest (who was rolled down the hill to his death in a nail-studded barrel in 1046 by pagans opposed to Christianity), it was previously known as Pest Hill, taking its name from the Slavic word for cave or oven (*pestj*), probably with reference to both the extensive karst cave system and to the hot thermal springs.

The sacred caves of the Greek island of Crete include several used for worship by the ancient Minoans (amongst them the Cave of Kamares, famous for its distinctive pottery), and the Cave of Agia Sophia, which has a small Christian church built inside the cave itself. Agia Sophia has an enormous cathedral-like chamber, and an impressive range of stalagmite and stalactite formations, some of them measuring up to 6 m. The best known of these is a rock and stalagmite formation that resembles a

John Spies explores the ancient caves of Tham Lod in Pang Mapha, Thailand.

unicorn. The cave is important for its geological formations, as a place of worship and also as a source of legend. One popular legend has it that the hoof-like imprint on a rock inside the cave (probably a rim pool) is that of St George's horse.

Similarly in Ethiopia two remarkable built-up cave churches, dating back to the Zagwe dynasty, which came to power in the eleventh century, were hidden in 'huge gaping cavern[s]' on spurs of the mountain Abuna Yosef.[10] Both Makina Madhane 'Alam (Church of the Redeemer) and Yemrehanna Krestos (named after the Zagwe king) are built structures located inside natural caves. Yemrehanna Krestos also contains a second, secular building, and has been used for centuries as a burial site.

The most significant of the many cave temples in Malaysia are undoubtedly the Batu Caves, situated in a towering limestone hill north of Kuala Lumpur. The main cave, known as Cathedral Cave or Temple Cave, is reached by climbing a steep flight of 272 steps and running a hazardous gauntlet of macaque monkeys. It, too, contains a built temple, the small Hindu shrine, established in 1891 and dedicated to Lord Murugan (Subramaniam), which has become a major destination for pilgrims (and tourists) particularly during the annual festival of Thaipusam (a festival of penance). Below the Temple Cave is the Dark Cave, the largest of the Batu Caves, a 2-km network of caverns containing elaborate formations such as cave curtains, flow stones, cave pearls and scallops; it, too, is open to the public.

Famous Buddhist caves in Burma include the labyrinthine Pindaya Cave on the Shan plateau, which contains over 8,000 images of the Buddha, the huge Saddan Cave in Kayin state, which houses a stupa and numerous buddhas and frescoes, and the nearby Kogun Cave where, as V. C. Scott O'Connor, then the British comptroller of Assam, wrote in *The Silken East* (1904):

> Ten thousand images of the Buddha lie within the first
> sweep of the eye, from yellow-robed figures which line the
> footpath, to terra-cotta plaques fixed high on the jutting face
> of the cliff; from golden colossi, twice the height of Goliath,
> to miniature figures fit for a penwiper. A great stalagmite,

rising up from the floor to near the brow of the overhanging cliff, is completely covered with small images of the Buddha enthroned, and its summit is crowned by a small pagoda.[11]

Hundreds of other caves in the region function as sacred sites. In Thailand alone it is estimated that over 200 caves are regularly used as places of Buddhist worship, including the impressive Tham Khao Luang which, like many other cave shrines in Thailand, is now also a firm fixture on the tourist trail.

Over the centuries the sublime, visual grandeur of caves has inspired religious awe around the world; in turn the awe which encouraged religious worship has stirred interest in sacred caves among the wider public, leading to many now being open not only as places of devotion, but as show caves. In some of the world's holy caves, the sacred has been joined or overtaken by the secular.

Stone Flower Cave (Shihua Dong), Fangshan, Beijing, China.

9 Extraordinary to Behold: Spectacular Caves

Cavers enter the darkness under the earth for 'beauty, adventure, mystery, comradeship'.[1] Tourists, however, flock in their millions to show caves around the world for beauty, perhaps for a touch of adventure or mystery and, increasingly, for a brush with science. So while the famous French caver Norbert Casteret can confidently assert that 'for a devoted and enthusiastic spelaeologist no cave is devoid of interest',[2] to interest the tourist a cave *must* be remarkable: it must, above all else, be a thing of beauty.

Show caves – or tourist caves as they are also called – are natural caves that are open to the public for an entry fee. They incorporate well-maintained passages and modern lighting systems that illuminate the way and highlight the cave's special features, and typically they offer guided tours that provide information about the history and geology of the cave. They are places where the interactions between humans and the caves are visibly managed (though less so in the case of adventure tourism). Increasingly, as conservation practices encourage us to tread lightly on the planet, there is a trend towards managing the cave rather than the visitor, placing greater importance on the preservation of the formations than on the experience of the more than twenty million tourists who visit show caves each year. But when and why did people begin to visit caves for tourism, rather than for shelter, ritual purposes or exploration?

Cave tourism dates back to the beginning of the sixteenth century when people began to visit the spectacular Postojnska jama in Slovenia on a regular basis (though there is graffiti

inside the cave which provides evidence of occasional visits dating back to 1213). The first show cave (determined by an entry fee) is the Vilenica jama, also in Slovenia, where the Count of Petac was charging an admission fee as early as 1633.[3] The first official cave guide is believed to have been Hans Jürgen Becker, who conducted tours of Baumann's Cave (Baumannshöhle) in Germany from 1668, while trained cave guides were employed at the Ojców caves in Poland from around 1810. John Hutton's *A Tour to the Caves, in the environs of Ingleborough and Settle, in the West-Riding of Yorkshire*, published in 1780, is one of the earliest cave guidebooks; many caves in central Europe were described in guidebooks for travellers during the Romantic period (roughly 1780–1848); and in 1801 the first written guide to show caves, Carl Lang's *Gallerie der unterirdischen Schöpfungs-Wunder und des menschlichen Kunstfleisses unter der Erde*, was published, with details of famous caves in Germany, Belgium, England, Portugal and Greece.

In the early nineteenth century some of the great tourist caves of the world, including Postojnska, Wookey Hole in Britain and Mammoth Cave in the United States, opened to

Postcard: 'Echo River, 360 ft underground in the Mammoth Cave of Kentucky.'

the public and the seemingly inexorable march towards the commercial show caves we know today began.

Postojnska jama – described by Johann Weichard von Valvasor in *Die Ehre des Hertzogthums Crain* in 1689 – was opened to the public in 1819, after a cave guide, Luka Čeč, had discovered extensive new parts of the cave the previous year. In 1823 Girolamo Agapito published the first guidebook to the cave system. The most significant development, however, took place in 1872 when rails were laid and the first cave train, originally pushed by the guides, began to carry tourists. The popularity of the cave at this time is demonstrated by the fact that electric lighting was installed in 1884, even before it was installed in Ljubljana, the provincial capital.

The Cheddar Caves in Somerset claim to be the first tourist show caves in Britain, with two then rival caves operating by the mid-nineteenth century: Cox's Cave, known to have been open to visitors in 1837; and Gough's Old Cave (also known as the Great Stalactite Cavern) which was operating as a show cave by 1869. Gough's New Cave, now known as Gough's Cave, explored between 1892 and 1898, was opened to visitors in 1899, and Gough's Old Cave was subsequently closed, though exactly when is not clear. The Great Stalactite Cavern, which could be visited for an admission fee of one shilling in 1869, was further developed following the discovery of new large chambers in 1877 and 1888. The cave was used regularly for entertainments with reports in the local press of a handbell concert in 1877 and a lantern slide show in 1881. Gas lighting was installed in 1883, walkways through the cave were improved, a tea garden was opened around 1885, and a small museum had been built by 1890. An acrostic written by Gough, which appears on a handbill advertising Gough's Old Cave, published around 1885, gives details of the admission charges at the time:

> Great and glorious are the sights seen here.
> Only one shilling to pay 'My pretty dear.'
> Unless you come by yourself, Thence
> Gough will charge you eighteen-pence.

Herein are seen great sights so rare.
So wonderful, 'twill make you stare.

Come one and all you'll enjoyment find –
And some of your cash leave behind:
Very great pleasure you'll obtain –
Enough I have said, so now refrain.[4]

Gough's (New) Cave, Cox's Cave and Wookey Hole were all visited by E. A. Martel during his trip to Britain in 1904. The Gough's Cave visitors' book contains the following entry for 15 June, signed by the famous speleologist-cum-tourist:

E. A. Martel and Madame (Paris)
Most pleased with Gough's cave, really very interesting as well on picturesque as on scientific points of view.[5]

By the middle of the century Kentucky's Mammoth Cave, which opened to the paying public in 1816, was being visited by tourists from around the world willing to put up with the difficulties of actually reaching the attraction. It was advertized as 'The Greatest Natural Curiosity in America' and an ideal summer resort, with the Cave Hotel (operated by the owners of the cave) able to accommodate up to 500 guests, who could avail themselves of the tours conducted by slaves of the cave owners. In his *Guide Manual to the Mammoth Cave of Kentucky*, published in 1860, Charles W. Wright describes in detail the many underground avenues then accessible to visitors, including the Main Cave and the twelve-hour 'Long Route'. Curiously he also offers advice on appropriate dress, giving us a good idea of what cave tourists would have looked like as they wandered through the subterranean passages 150 years ago:

The proper costume for a gentleman consists of a jacket, heavy boots, and a cloth cap.
    The Bloomer or Turkish dress is the proper costume for a lady. It may be plain, or fancifully trimmed, to suit

the wearer. When trimmed in lively colors, which is always advisable, the effect is beautiful, particularly if the party be large. Flannel or cloth is the proper material. It must be borne in mind that the temperature in the Cave is fifty-nine degrees.

Every lady carries a lamp, and in no case, except that of illness, should she take a gentleman's arm. It is fatiguing to both parties, and exceedingly awkward in appearance.[6]

Whether cave tourists in Australia were so well turned out for their subterranean excursions is not clear, but visits to caves were increasingly popular by the 1860s. Although there were irregular guided tours of Chudleigh Caves in Tasmania following their discovery in the early 1830s (Anthony Trollope, who visited the caves in 1872, described them as 'one of the wonders of Tasmania'),[7] the Jenolan Caves in New South Wales are undoubtedly the birthplace of the Australian show cave industry. The commercial history of Jenolan Caves dates back to the 1861 visit of the local politician John Lucas (who did much to ensure the preservation of the fragile cave environment, and after whom the Lucas Cave is named). In 1866 the Jenolan Caves Reserve was proclaimed and Jeremiah Wilson was appointed its first keeper the following year. As more caves were discovered and visitor numbers grew, so did

Show Caves:
Entrance Tickets.

the commercial development both outside and within the attraction. In the 1880s accommodation was built for visitors, while inside the caves pathways were constructed, wire protection was introduced to prevent further damage to the already vandalized speleothems, and permanent electric lights were installed in 1887. By the end of the nineteenth century Jenolan Caves were well established as one of the major tourist destinations in Australia.

Even as show caves continued to open around the world in the early decades of the twentieth century, it was becoming clear that the enormous success of the industry was not without its problems. As Elery Hamilton-Smith explains, 'The cave tourism experience became remarkably stereotyped, with visitors being grouped into parties, each led through brightly lit caves along fixed pathways by a talking guide.'[8] Although pathways were upgraded, better lighting was installed and the presentation and interpretation of the cave formations improved, with some notable exceptions the cave tourism experience itself changed little until late in the century.

In 1989 the British Association of Show Caves (BAS) was established as an umbrella organization for show cave operators in Britain; it was expanded in 2001 to include leading show caves in Ireland and renamed the Association of British and Irish Show Caves (ABIS). Current members are Cheddar Cave, Ingleborough Cave, Kents Cavern, Peak Cavern, Poole's Cavern, Stump Cross Caverns, Treak Cliff Cavern and Wookey Hole in England; Marble Arch Caves in Northern Ireland; Dan-yr-Ogof (National Showcaves Centre for Wales) in Wales; and Aillwee Cave, Crag Cave, Doolin Cave, Dunmore Cave and Mitchelstown Cave in Ireland. The association and its members are committed to providing visitors with an understanding of the geology, archaeology and cultural history of their underground sites to complement the visual feast of the cave formations themselves, while also ensuring that the cave environments are properly managed and protected. Well-laid paths, discreet lighting and informed guides (or audio guides) providing scientific as well as cultural commentary are common

'Queen Victoria's Bloomers', Ingleborough Cave, Yorkshire.

to many of the caves, as are the improved facilities for visitors which now often include tea rooms and shops selling a range of souvenirs, from guidebooks and postcards to mugs and pin badges. The glossy souvenir booklets available at many of these show caves offer the tourist a concise introduction to cave science, from the formation of solution caves to geological history, alongside the exploration and cultural history of the cave.

But the experience of visiting the various caves is now not by any means a uniform one. Ingleborough Cave, for example, continues to operate as a very traditional show cave. The hourlong return journey relies on the beauty of the site's natural features, including a spectacular pair of stalactites known as

Queen Victoria's Bloomers, to satisfy its visitors. (The guides claim the royal moniker caused Queen Victoria to halt a knighthood intended for the local landowner, James Farrer.) Both Peak Cavern, with the largest natural cave entrance in the British Isles, and White Scar Cave, the longest show cave in Britain, also rely on a traditional tour by well-informed and entertaining guides. Peak Cavern supplements its tour with a demonstration of traditional rope making in the cave entrance, and additionally caters for functions (such as medieval banquets) in the cave as well as staging various musical events including a carol concert each Christmas in the natural amphitheatre of the cave entrance. The tour of the Marble Arch Caves in Northern Ireland, though largely traditional in its approach, is augmented by a short trip along the cave's subterranean river aboard an electrically powered boat, and an audio-visual presentation in the visitor centre. Significantly, this show cave is a key site in the UNESCO-endorsed Marble Arch Caves Global Geopark, and as such places a high value on conservation and science. Similarly Kents Cavern, a protected national site and a gateway visitor centre for UNESCO's English Riviera Global Geopark, prioritizes the rich geology and archaeological heritage of the cave alongside the visitor experience which now includes a range of events from a Stone Age woodland trail to regular 'Shakespeare Underground' performances. The Dan-yr-Ogof Caves, the National Showcaves Centre for Wales, have moved as far from the traditional model as any show cave in Britain and Ireland. The three caves open to visitors for self-guided tours (which include information for the scientifically curious) cannot be visited without purchasing a ticket to the Centre, a theme park which includes ten attractions ranging from a model Iron Age village to a dinosaur park with life-sized models to a shire horse centre, and organizes weddings for those inclined to be married underground in front of family, friends and random cave tourists. Dinosaurs are also one of the attractions at the Wookey Hole theme park, where again the cave tour is only one of the several activities on offer, and visitors wishing to see

Aven Armand, France.

Dobšinská Ice Cave, Slovakia.

Gough's Cave or Cox's Cave must buy a Cheddar Gorge and Caves Explorer ticket, which also includes entry to the Crystal Quest fantasy adventure, the Cheddar Man Museum and the Lookout Tower, as well as a clifftop Gorge walk and an open-top bus tour. At these three sites, and others, the show caves are part of a family day out, rather than a specific attraction in themselves. Dedicated show cave tourists in Britain, it seems, must increasingly look north to Derbyshire and Yorkshire for less adulterated underground experiences.

Elsewhere in Europe there have been many significant, and sometimes unusual, technical developments in the show cave industry over the last hundred years. Austria's Eisriesenwelt, the largest natural limestone ice cave in the world, was developed as a show cave in the 1920s, with a cable car built in 1955 to improve access to it. There is no electric light in the cave; instead, visitors carry carbide lamps, with the most spectacular forms being illuminated by magnesium ribbon. The 1920s also saw the development of the Aven Armand in France, with, since 1963, visitors descending into the cavern in a funicular. The Ochtinská Aragonite Cave in Slovakia, discovered in the late nineteenth century, is the only crystal show

'Mammoth Cave diptych', Mammoth Cave, Kentucky.

Grand Avenue Tour, Mammoth Cave, Kentucky.

cave in Europe. It was opened to the public in 1972 and placed on the UNESCO World Heritage List in 1995. The development of Postojnska jama, an important biospeleological centre as well as the most visited show cave in Europe, has continued through the twentieth and into the twenty-first century, with over five of more than 20 km of interwoven passages and chambers now open to the public. Most notably, the rail system used to carry visitors into the cave has been modernized on several occasions, with a two-track railway and battery-powered engine being introduced in 1963. Visitors are now whisked deep inside the earth by train to where they continue their guided tour on foot, ending up in the huge Concert Hall which houses a souvenir shop and can accommodate an audience of several thousand for special events.

Snowball Dining Room, Mammoth Cave, Kentucky.

While cave tourists usually visit caves to see their spectacular geological formations, they flock to the Blue Grotto (Grotta Azzurra), a sea cave on the coast of the Italian island of Capri, to see the brilliant deep blue light that floods the roomy chamber through an underground entrance. Whether they approach the grotto by land or sea, all tourists must enter the cave lying on their backs in one of the small wooden boats that ferry visitors through the small entranceway to the cave.

The development of Kentucky's Mammoth Cave, the longest known cave in the world, as a show cave through the twentieth century and into the twenty-first has been balanced with the need to protect the scientific value of the cave. The Mammoth Cave National Park was established in 1941 (the same year the National Speleological Society was founded) and designated a World Heritage Site 40 years later for its geological, archaeological and biological significance. The Park's support for conservation, research and environmentally sound economic growth was further recognized in 1990 when it was designated an International Biosphere Reserve. Mammoth Cave, the 'stellar attraction'[9] of the Park, now has 15 km of underground trails open to the public and offers sixteen tours. These range from the short self-guided Mammoth Cave Discovery Tour to the strenuous four-and-a-half-hour Grand Avenue Tour. There are also a number of speciality tours including the historic Violet City Lantern Tour conducted by lantern light. The group sizes at this immensely popular show cave, which range from 30 on the speciality Focus on Frozen Niagara Photo tour to 120 on the classic Historic Tour, give some idea of the sheer volume of tourist traffic that passes through the cave each day, and the potential damage that could occur if the cave was not sympathetically managed. Visitors can augment their appetite for science, whetted on the tours, by collecting free brochures on the archaeology of Mammoth Cave, on biology and cave life, and on karst geology, as well as other cultural and historical topics.

The Kartchner Caverns, developed using the concept of 'conservation through commercialization',[10] set new standards for high-tech, science-informed management of show caves when they were opened to the public in 1999, 25 years after they had been discovered by Gary Tenen and Randy Tufts. The full story of the discovery and preservation of these caves is recounted in Neil Miller's book *Kartchner Caverns: How Two*

WELCOME TO

NEWDEGATE CAVE

HASTINGS CAVES STATE RESERVE

Visitors to the cave are required to observe the following ethics:

- Not to touch any rock or cave formation.
- Not to interfere with cave animals.
- Smoking is not permitted within the cave.
- Food or drink is not permitted within the cave.
- Litter should be placed in the bin outside the cave entrance.
- Tripods are not permitted in the cave. (The use of cameras and flashlights are permitted from cave pathways. However, please be considerate not to hold up the tour party.)
- Please remain with the guided party.

Thank you for your cooperation.

**Director
National Parks and Wildlife**

Parks and Wildlife Service

Cavers Discovered and Saved One of the Wonders of the Natural World (2008). After discovering the pristine caves in 1974, Tenen and Tufts kept the location secret for fourteen years. They decided that the best way to preserve the caves was to develop them as a tour cave, and in 1978 approached the Kartchner family who owned the land. In 1984 Tenen and Tufts and the Kartchner family agreed to approach the Arizona State Parks for assistance; in 1985 Governor Bruce Babbitt was taken on a tour of the cave; and in 1988 State Parks leased the property and the secret was out. It took another decade of meticulous planning and construction before the caves were ready to open to the public.

Cave ethics, signage at Newdegate Cave, Tasmania.

Two tours – the Rotunda/Throne Room tour and the Big Room tour (added in 2003) – are open to the public in carefully managed, small groups; both need to be booked well in advance, and visitors are required to observe the strict rules set out on the Caverns' website:

The following are NOT permitted on Cave Tours:
- Purses, handbags, backpacks, fanny packs, baby backpacks or other bags/items.
- Binoculars or flashlights.
- Photography or video equipment (to include phones, other electronic recording devices and tripods).
- Food, gum, tobacco products and drinks (including bottled water).

Embroidered patch for the Carlsbad Caverns, New Mexico.

- Strollers, walkers, crutches.
- Touching or damaging formations (punishable by law).
- Littering or tossing coins.[11]

Whereas most of the world's tourist caves show signs of the damage caused by visitors over the years, the Kartchner Caverns provide an opportunity to see a cave in a near pristine state. To do this the management goes to enormous lengths to minimize 'the contaminating effect of visitors' in a bid to maintain the cave's unspoilt environment.[12] Visitors enter the cave through a series of airlocks and pass through a water mist designed to settle the dust and lint they carry in on their bodies and clothes; the pathways inside the cave are hosed down each day to remove hair, skin cells and other body litter shed by visitors, as well as the vast amount of lint left behind from clothes; and each day the water in the cave is pumped out, filtered and returned as mist to maintain humidity levels and the moist cave atmosphere.[13] At Kartchner Caverns, while the tourist experience is important, it is not paramount; conservation and science come first.

Some remarkable show caves have been developed in karst regions across Asia since the middle of the last century, though sadly many others have opened with scant regard to conservation.

Reed Flute Cave, Guilin, China.

The Kong Lor Cave in Laos offers tourists a 7.5-km underground boat ride; the tourist route into Akiyoshi-do Cave in Japan takes visitors past a complex of 500 terraced rimstone pools as well as large stalagmites and columns; and four show caves are now open in Malaysia's Gunung Mulu National Park in Sarawak, including Deer Cave, the largest cave passage in the world, where visitors can watch the nightly exodus of the approximately three million wrinkled-lipped bats that live in the cave (and lend it a particularly pungent aroma), vividly captured in the 'Caves' episode of the BBC documentary series *Planet Earth* (2006).

In China there are about 200 show caves currently open to tourists, many of them in the karst regions of Guizhou, Guangxi, Hunan, Yunnan and Zhejiang provinces. The development of show caves in China has followed the global pattern of guided tour groups being led along concrete pathways through brightly lit caves. Some, like the Reed Flute Cave (Ludi Cave) near Guilin in Guangxi province, offer additional events such as underground dinners. This cave and the nearby Returned Pearl Cave inspired the Australian Aboriginal poet Oodgeroo Noonuccal (Kath Walker) during her visit in 1984:

I think I saw
A dragon with a pearl in his mouth,
Fly out of the cave[14]

And in 'Reed Flute Cave', where she is unexpectedly reminded of Aboriginal Dreamtime, she highlights the storytelling potential of cave formations:

mushrooms and every type of fruit,
vegetable, animal and fish
Are on display.[15]

While electric lighting in the majority of caves in Europe and the United States comes on only intermittently and is relatively muted to minimize the growth of algae and to show off the caves in as natural a way as possible (given that there is no natural way to see a cave in absolute darkness), unnatural coloured lights and bright neon signs invariably greet the cave tourist in China. The Stone Flower Cave (Shihua Dong) near Beijing is one of the biggest Chinese show caves. Four of the eight levels are now open to visitors, who descend 150 m beneath the surface and walk 2.5 km through sixteen halls during their two-hour underground tour. The well-preserved speleothems include huge stalactites and stalagmites, two stone shields, a stone flag and a large stone curtain. The whole breathtaking experience is illuminated by a fairyland of coloured lights that lends a surreal atmosphere to the spectacle.

In Australia the Jenolan Caves, which attract over 250,000 visitors each year, are a good example of the way tourism can sit comfortably alongside exploration, technical innovation and scientific research in show caves. Ten caves have been developed and are open for regular tours: Lucas Cave; River Cave; Chifley Cave (known as the Left Imperial Cave until 1952); Imperial Cave; Orient Cave; Ribbon Cave; Pool of Cerberus Cave; Jubilee Cave; Temple of Baal Cave; and Nettle Cave. The Lucas Cave tour, which can accommodate up to 65 people, remains the most popular; the centrepiece of the tour, the large Cathedral Chamber, is also used for weddings and regular concerts. At the other end of the spectrum the Pool of Cerberus tour caters for a maximum of only eight people. All except the Nettle Cave tour are guided. Nettle Cave, which was closed to the public in 1932, was reopened for self-guided tours in 2006, with the commentary available in eleven languages (including Klingon!). In common with several tourist caves around the world, including America's Kartchner Caverns, Jenolan has a historical society – the Jenolan Caves Historical and Preservation Society – which has its own website and publishes occasional papers and booklets as well as a quarterly newsletter. Research carried out by scientists from the Commonwealth Scientific and Industrial Research Organisation (CSIRO), the Australian Museum and Sydney University, in cooperation with the Jenolan Caves Trust, has shown that the Jenolan Caves date back more than 340 million

Tin of taro sticks from the Silver Cave, Yangshuo County, China.

years, making it the oldest-known cave system in the world.[16]

Many of these twentieth-century developments are variations on the traditional show caves theme: improvements in guided (and self-guided) tours, infrastructure, lighting and facilities for special events; greater research links and opportunities; the introduction of transport inside caves; and add-on activities outside the caves. Some of these 'artificial entertainments', as Hamilton-Smith calls them, 'unless they are of outstanding merit . . . probably do more to detract from the

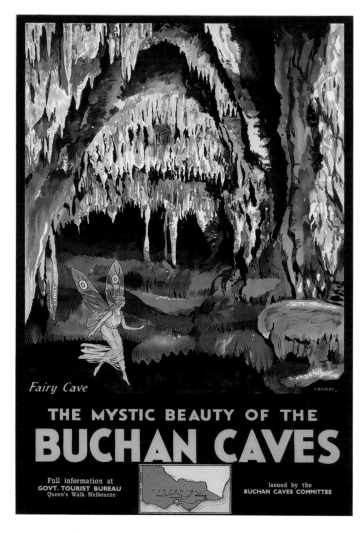

Fairy Cave

THE MYSTIC BEAUTY OF THE
BUCHAN CAVES

Full information at
GOVT. TOURIST BUREAU
Queen's Walk. Melbourne

Issued by the
BUCHAN CAVES COMMITTEE

natural values of the cave than to accentuate them'.[17] This is
noticeably the case where multi-attraction theme parks have
been developed around show caves.

As the twenty-first century progresses, the big change
sweeping through the tourist cave industry is the advent of
adventure caving. A number of show caves around the world
have now extended their activities to include adventure caving
in some form. At one end of the scale, Aven Armand offers

more adventurous tourists the option of abseiling down the natural shaft used by the explorers Louis Armand and Martel, who discovered the cave in 1897, before joining those who descended in the funicular to continue their guided tour. At the other end of the scale, Mammoth Cave's Wild Cave Tour is a far more demanding underground challenge which takes a small group of up to fourteen tourists on a strenuous six-and-a-half-hour, 8-km journey underground, and includes lengthy crawls through tight passages. Jenolan Caves now offers visitors a choice of four award-winning adventure tours that range in degree of difficulty from the introductory Plughole Adventure Tour, which includes abseiling and squeezes, through to the technically advanced Central River Adventure Tour, designed for the most daring (and experienced) adventure cave tourists, with muddy passages, demanding climbs, squeezes, twisting rockpiles and two underground abseil pitches included in the seven-hour trip. In Tasmania, visitors to Mole Creek can choose to follow the floodlit concrete path into the wonderland of the Marakoopa and King Solomon's show caves, or to venture into one of the undeveloped Mole Creek caves on a Wild Cave Tour. In New Zealand – which has long been in the vanguard of adventure tourism – there are numerous caving adventure experiences on offer for adrenaline junkies. In the Waitomo area, home to the world famous Waitomo Glowworm Caves, the Ruakiri Cave (New Zealand's longest guided underground tour) and the Aranui Cave, thrill-seeking visitors can choose from a wide range of subterranean adventure tours that offer activities such as cave tubing (blackwater rafting), abseiling, climbing, underground flying foxes and, on Waitomo Adventures' wonderfully named Haggas Honking Holes tour, the promise to make visitors 'feel like Indiana Jones in a washing machine'.[18] Many of these tours also have a strong educational focus, with guides sharing their knowledge of history and geology or other sciences along the way.

One consequence of the development of adventure cave tours has been to blur the use of the terms show cave and tourist cave. Tourist caves, like show caves, charge an entrance fee, and the tours are guided; but the caves themselves can be undeveloped, or only minimally developed to ameliorate safety standards, without the lights, pathways or interpretation that are the common hallmarks of show caves. A show cave is always a tourist cave, but a tourist cave is not always a show cave.

As cave exploration spawned an interest in cave tourism in the nineteenth century, so now in the twenty-first century cave tourism is completing the circle and introducing tourists to the sport of caving, to exploration and, through a range of education programmes, to cave science. Approaches to the management of caves have changed and developed, too. Moves towards a holistic cave management model – providing greater environmental protection for the caves – has led to an increasing distance between the cave and its human tourist visitors. Counter to this, the development of adventure cave tourism has successfully produced the fiction that the human tourists are experiencing an authentic encounter with a wild cave.

As the boundaries of cave tourism continue to be pushed in the future, interest in caves can only grow.

NOTABLE CAVES

Abîme de Bramabiau: Edouard-Alfred Martel's through-crossing of the plateau de Camprieu in southern France via the underground river of the Abîme de Bramabiau on 28 June 1888 is regarded by many as the birth of modern speleology.

Actun Tunichil Muknal (Cave of the Stone Sepulchre, also known as Xibalba) in Belize is an important Mayan archaeological site; it contains a sacrificial chamber where human remains have been found, along with pottery vessels permanently embedded in the cave's formations.

Altamira Cave near Santander in Spain is often referred to as the Sistine Chapel of cave art for the paintings of wild animals and human hands that decorate its chambers, dating back over 15,000 years to the Upper Palaeolithic period (50,000 to 10,000 years ago). Altamira II, a facsimile of the original cave, was opened a few hundred metres away in 2001.

Aven Armand in the Lozère département, France, discovered by Edouard Martel and Louis Armand in 1897, has been open to the public since 1927. Since 1963 visitors have been able to descend into the cavern in a funicular.

Aven d'Orgnac in the Ardèche region of France, discovered by Robert de Joly in 1935 and open to the public since 1939, is the only cave system granted 'Grand Site de France' status.

Barton Creek Cave, Cayo, Belize, is a popular tourist cave and an important Mayan archaeological site. Human remains and pottery shards dating back to 200 CE have been found in the cave.

Batu Caves temple complex, north of Kuala Lumpur, is one of the most important Hindu shrines outside India. The largest cave, known as

Temple Cave or Cathedral Cave, houses an ornate shrine and is reached by climbing a steep flight of 272 steps.

Blue holes of the Bahamas are spectacular underwater caves named for the deep blue colour of the water. There are estimated to be over 1,000 blue holes in the Bahamas.

Boesmansgat (Bushman's Hole), Northern Cape Province, South Africa, at approximately 270 m deep is one of the world's deepest freshwater caves. The site of a number of cave-diving records, the cave has also claimed the lives of several divers.

Cango Caves in South Africa's Western Cape, believed to have been discovered in the late eighteenth century, are among the country's most popular tourist caves.

Cave of Swimmers in the Gilf Kebir region of the Sahara Desert is named for the prehistoric drawings of swimming figures that adorn its walls. It features prominently in Michael Ondaatje's novel *The English Patient* (1992).

Chauvet Cave, France, discovered in 1994, is the subject of Werner Herzog's 3D documentary film *Cave of Forgotten Dreams*. In order to prevent damage to its remarkable cave art, it has never been open to the public.

Cheddar Caves in Somerset comprise Cox's Cave, discovered in 1837, and Gough's Cave, the most visited show cave in Britain, discovered in 1893.

Corycian Cave is located on Mount Parnassus, Greece. According to mythology the cave is named for the nymph Corycia, and is sacred to the god Pan.

Cueva de las Velas (Cave of Crystals), Mexico, situated 300 m below Chihuahua's Naica Mine, is famous for the gigantic selenite crystals found in its main chamber.

Dent de Crolles system near Grenoble, France, was extensively explored between 1936 and 1947 by a team of cavers that included Pierre Chevalier and Fernand Petzl. At 658 m it was the world's deepest explored cave at that time.

Eisriesenwelt Cave, Werfen, Austria, is considered the world's largest ice cave. Formed by natural limestone ice and over 42 km long, it attracts more than 200,000 visitors annually.

Fingal's Cave, on the Scottish island of Staffa, is a cathedral-like cave with distinctive hexagonal basalt columns. It inspired numerous nine-teenth-century artists, including Felix Mendelssohn, whose visit in 1829 inspired the work popularly known as the *Fingal's Cave* overture.

Flint Ridge Cave System, Kentucky, was connected to Mammoth Cave in 1972, making the Mammoth-Flint Ridge Cave System the longest in the world.

Gaping Ghyll in Yorkshire, at 109.7 m (360 ft), is the deepest cave shaft in Britain. The Gaping Ghyll winch, which operates twice a year, enables non-cavers to visit the cavern floor.

Gouffre Berger, France, discovered in 1953, at 1,112 m, was for ten years regarded as the deepest cave in the world. The cave has claimed the lives of six cavers in recent years, five of the fatalities caused by sudden violent flooding.

Gouffre de Padirac in the Lot region, first descended by Edouard Martel in 1889, is now the most visited tourist cave in France.

Grotta Azzurra (Blue Grotto), a sea cave on the coast of Capri, Italy, is famous for the deep blue light that floods the chamber through an underwater cavity.

Hang Don Doong, Quang Binh, Vietnam, discovered by Howard and Deb Limbert in 2009, is one of the largest caves in the world.

Jeita Grotto, Lebanon, is a system of two interconnected caves, the upper cave of which contains what is believed to be the world's largest known stalactite. Inhabited in prehistoric times, the cave is now one of Lebanon's top tourist attractions.

Jenolan Caves, New South Wales, Australia, is the oldest known cave system in the world. Much of the extensive system is accessible only to cavers, but ten caves have been developed for tourism and are visited by over 250,000 people each year.

Kartchner Caverns in Arizona was discovered in 1974 by Gary Tenen and Randy Tufts, who kept the location secret for fourteen years.

Opened to the public in 1999, the caves set new standards for
high-tech, conservation management of show caves.

Kazumura Cavern, Hawaii, the longest continuous lava tube in the
world, was formed between 400 and 600 years ago following the
eruption of a vent on the side of the volcano Kilauea Caldera.

Krubera Cave in Abkhazia, Georgia, at 2,197 m, is the deepest known
cave in the world. Cavers have likened the descent into Krubera to
climbing an inverted Mount Everest.

Lascaux Cave near Montignac in southern France is famous for its
Palaeolithic cave paintings of animals which date back more than 15,000
years. Opened as a tourist cave in 1948, it was closed to the public in
1963 to prevent further damage to the art. Lascaux II, a facsimile cave
which exactly replicates key features, was opened nearby in 1983.

Lechuguilla Cave, located in Carlsbad Caverns National Park, New
Mexico, is the fifth-longest cave in the world. It is famous for its rare
speleothems with large amounts of gypsum and sulphur deposits. Access
is limited to scientific research, survey and exploration teams.

Majlis al Jinn Cave, located in the Selma Plateau, Oman, was
considered the world's second largest cave chamber in terms of the
surface area of the floor when it was surveyed in 1985, though several
larger chambers have since been surveyed.

Mammoth Cave in Kentucky, part of the Mammoth-Flint Ridge Cave
System, the longest in the world, has been open to visitors since 1816.
It was extensively mapped in 1842 by the slave Stephen Bishop, who
worked as a guide in the cave in the 1840s and 1850s.

Marble Arch Caves in Co. Fermanagh, Northern Ireland, is a key site in
the UNESCO-endorsed Marble Arch Caves Global Geopark. Electrically
powered boats transport visitors along its subterranean river.

Mulu Caves, in Sarawak's Gunung Mulu National Park, Malaysia, are
among the most spectacular in the world. Extensively explored since
1978, recent expeditions have confirmed the Sarawak Chamber as the
world's largest underground chamber, and Deer Cave as the largest
known cave passage.

Naracoorte Caves in South Australia have acted as pitfall traps for over
500,000 years, providing Australia's most complete fossil record. The

caves were placed on the UNESCO World Heritage List in 1994 in recognition of the importance of the fossils in the cave, including megafauna such as the wombat-like diprotodon, the marsupial lion and giant kangaroos.

Newdegate Cave in Tasmania, the largest dolomite show cave in Australia, is part of the Hastings Caves State Reserve.

Ochtinská Aragonite Cave in Slovakia, discovered in the late nineteenth century, is the only crystal show cave in Europe. It was opened to the public in 1972 and placed on the UNESCO World Heritage List in 1995.

Paroong Cave, South Australia, contains some of the best examples of Aboriginal Karake art, which is characterized by engravings cut deep into the cave walls.

Peak Cavern, one of four show caves in Castleton, Derbyshire, is the largest in the Peak District. Also known as 'Devil's Arse', its main entrance, which is the largest natural cave entrance in the British Isles, was home to 'troglodytes' until 1915.

Postojnska jama, opened to the public in 1819, is one of Slovenia's top tourist sites and one of the best-known show caves in the world; the first cave train began operating here in 1872, and electric lighting was added in 1884.

Puerto Princesa Underground River Cave in the Philippines contains a huge 300-m cave dome and an 8.2-km underground river that flows directly into the South China Sea.

Reed Flute Cave, Guilin, China, is one of the tourist highlights in a region known for its extraordinary karst topography. Its impressive formations are illuminated by multicoloured lighting, common in Chinese show caves, and 70 inscriptions on the cave walls can be dated back as far as the Tang Dynasty, *c.* 792 CE.

Sistema Dos Ojos (Two Eyes), Cenotes Park, Mexico, comprises two cenotes (sinkholes created by the collapse of cave ceilings) that open onto the same large cavern. The flooded cave system, discovered in the late 1980s, is still one of the longest known underwater cave systems in the world. A number of documentaries and films, including *The Cave* (2005), have been shot here.

Skocjan Caves, Slovenia, is one of the longest karst underground wetlands in Europe. It is noted for the huge volume of its underground channel, and for the size of some of its underground chambers, including Martel's Chamber, one of the largest underground chambers in Europe.

Sof Omar Caves is the longest cave system in Ethiopia and possibly Africa. Sacred to both Islam and the local Oromo religion, the caves are also known for the cluster of thick columns found in the Chamber of Columns.

Three Counties System extends under Cumbria, Lancashire and Yorkshire. The final connection in the interconnecting caves was made in 2011, opening up the longest cave network in Britain.

Waitomo Caves, situated in the Waikato, New Zealand, include Ruakuri Cave and Aranui Cave, and the world-famous Glow-worm Cave, named for the tiny glow worms, Arachnocampa Luminosa, endemic to New Zealand, that are found in large numbers in the cave.

Wargata Mina (Judds Cavern), in Tasmania's Cracroft Valley, is one of the longest river caves in Australia; a large chamber is decorated with Tasmanian Aboriginal rock art, twenty stencils and red ochre smears dating back to the Ice Age.

White Scar Caves, Yorkshire, the longest show cave in Britain, was discovered by Christopher Long in 1923. Its attractions include waterfalls, flowstone terraces and the huge Battlefield Cavern, one of the largest caverns in the country.

REFERENCES

1 What is a Cave?

1 C.H.D. Cullingford, ed., *British Caving: An Introduction to Speleology* (London, 1953), p. 4.
2 Arthur N. Palmer, *Cave Geology* (Dayton, OH, 2007), p. 1.
3 Adrienne Eberhard, 'Earth, Air, Water, Fire: A Love Poem in Four Elements', in *This Woman* (North Fitzroy, VIC, 2011), p. 86.
4 David Poyer, *Down to a Sunless Sea* (New York, 1998), p. 3.
5 David Gillieson, *Caves: Processes, Development, Management* (Oxford, 1996), p. 3; Robert Penn Warren, *The Cave* (London, 1959), p. 179.
6 Michael Ray Taylor, *Cave Passages: Roaming the Underground Wilderness* (New York, 1996), p. 103.
7 Ibid., p. 107.
8 Greg Garrard, *Ecocriticism* (London, 2004), p. 4.
9 Plato, *The Republic* (Harmondsworth, 1987), p. 317.
10 Ibid., p. 318.
11 Ibid., p. 318.
12 Ibid., pp. 320–21, 324.
13 Sigmund Freud, *The Interpretation of Dreams* [1899] (London, 1997), p. 233.
14 See Meredith Sabini, 'The Bones in the Cave: Phylogenic Foundations of Analytical Psychology', *Journal of Jungian Theory and Practice*, II/2 (2000), p. 19.
15 Arne Naess, 'The Deep Ecology Movement: Some Philosophical Aspects', in *Deep Ecology for the 21st Century: Readings on the Philosophy and Practice of the New Environmentalism*, ed. George Sessions (Boston, MA, 1995), p. 68.
16 Gillieson, *Caves*, p. 1.
17 Garrard, *Ecocriticism*, p. 70.
18 Barbara Hurd, *Entering the Stone: On Caves and Feeling through the Dark* (Athens, GA, 2008), p. 35.
19 George Crothers, P. Willey and Patty Jo Watson, 'Cave Archaeo-

logy and the NSS: 1941–2006', *Journal of Cave and Karst Studies*, LXIX/1 (2007), p. 29.
20 Warren, *The Cave*, p. 191.
21 Nevada Barr, *Blind Descent* (New York, 2009), p. 24.
22 Sherod Santos, 'Fermanagh Cave', in *The Pilot Star Elegies* (New York, 1999), pp. 44–6.
23 John Freeman, 'The Caves', in *Poems New and Old* (London, 1920), p. 30.
24 Gillieson, *Caves*, pp. 59–60.

2 Speaking of Speleology

1 E. A. Martel, 'Speleology, or Cave Exploration', *Appleton's Popular Science Monthly*, LIV (1899), p. 255.
2 Quoted in Trevor Shaw, 'Speleologists', in *Encyclopedia of Caves and Karst Science*, ed. John Gunn (New York, 2004), p. 688.
3 Shaw, 'Speleologists', p. 687.
4 W. Boyd Dawkins, *Cave Hunting: Researches on the Evidence of Caves Respecting the Early Inhabitants of Europe* (London, 1874), p. 3.
5 Ibid., pp. 14–15.
6 Ibid., p. 8.
7 George Hartwig, *The Subterranean World* (London, 1871) pp. v–vi.
8 Ibid., p. v.
9 C.H.D. Cullingford, ed., *British Caving: An Introduction to Speleology* (London, 1953), p. 1.
10 Ibid., p. 3.
11 T. D. Ford and C.H.D. Cullingford, eds, *The Science of Speleology* (London, 1976), p. ix.
12 Philip LaMoreaux, 'Foreword', in *Encyclopedia of Caves*, ed. David C. Culver and William B. White (Burlington, MA, 2005), pp. xvii–xviii.
13 Patricia Kambesis, 'The Importance of Cave Exploration to Scientific Research', *Journal of Cave and Karst Studies*, LXIX/1 (2007), p. 46.
14 Arthur N. Palmer, *Cave Geology* (Dayton, OH, 2007), p. v.
15 Amitav Ghosh, *The Hungry Tide* (Delhi, 2004), p. 224.
16 William B. White and David C. Culver, 'Cave, Definition of', in *Encyclopedia of Caves*, ed. Culver and White, p. 82.
17 David Gillieson, *Caves: Processes, Development, Management* (Oxford, 1996), p. 5.
18 John Freeman, 'The Caves', in *Poems New and Old* (London, 1920), p. 30.
19 Palmer, *Cave Geology*, p. 11.

20 Ibid., p. 15.
21 William B. White, 'A Brief History of Karst Hydrogeology: Contributions of the NSS', *Journal of Cave and Karst Studies*, LXIX/1 (2007), p. 15.
22 Ibid.
23 Ibid.
24 Ibid.
25 Robert A. Heinlein. *Citizen of the Galaxy* [1957] (New York, 2005), p. 47.
26 Gillieson, *Caves*, pp. 105–6.
27 Mark Twain, *The Adventures of Tom Sawyer*, ed. Peter Stoneley (Oxford, 2008), pp. 186–7.
28 John Fowles, 'The Nature of Nature', in *Wormholes: Essays and Occasional Writings* (London, 1998), p. 358.
29 Judith Beveridge, 'How to Love Bats', in *Accidental Grace* (St Lucia, QLD, 1996), pp. 58–60.

3 Troglodytes and Troglobites: Living in the Dark Zone

1 Herodotus, *The Histories*, trans. Aubrey de Sélincourt (London, 2003), pp. 303–4.
2 David Kempe, *Living Underground: A History of Cave and Cliff Dwelling* (London, 1988), p. 125.
3 Hein Bjartmann Bjerck, 'On the Outer Fringe of the Human World: Phenomenological Perspectives on Anthropomorphic Cave Paintings in Norway', in *Caves in Context: The Cultural Significance of Caves and Rockshelters in Europe*, ed. Knut Andreas Bergsvik and Robin Skeates (Oxford, 2012), pp. 58–9.
4 Quoted in Tom Tyler, 'Four Hands Good, Two Hands Bad', in *Kafka's Creatures: Animals, Hybrids, and Other Fantastic Beings*, ed. Marc Lucht and Donna Yarri (Lanham, MD, 2010), p. 180.
5 While the term 'troglodyte' does not appear in Wells's novel – the narrator refers to them as 'Under-grounders' – it has become the standard term for the Morlocks in discussion of the novel.
6 H. G. Wells, *The Time Machine* [1895] (London, 2007), p. 51.
7 Ibid., pp. 49, 51, 45.
8 Knut Andreas Bergsvik and Robin Skeates, 'Caves in Context: An Introduction', in *Caves in Context*, ed. Bergsvik and Skeates, p. 8.
9 Cormac McCarthy, *The Road* (London, 2007), p. 1.
10 Ibid., p. 300.
11 See Bernard Rudofsky, *Architecture without Architects: A Short Introduction to Non-Pedigreed Architecture* (Albuquerque, NM, 1967), p. 8.
12 Galena Hashhozheva, 'Negative Architecture: Underground

Building in Gabriel Tarde and Thomas Pynchon', in *Between Science and Fiction: The Hollow Earth as Concept and Conceit*, ed. Hanjo Berressem, Michael Bucher and Uwe Schwagmeier (Berlin, 2012), p. 98.

13 Ibid., p. 98.

14 Max Moseley, 'Size Matters: Scalar Phenomena and a Proposal for an Ecological Definition of a Cave', *Cave and Karst Science*, XXXV/3 (2008), p. 89.

15 Xavier Belles, 'From Dragons to Allozymes: A Brief Account on the History of Biospeleology', in *The Natural History of Biospeleology*, ed. Ana Isabel Camacho (Madrid, 1994), p. 9.

16 Ana Isabel Camacho, 'Preface', in *The Natural History of Biospeleology*, ed. Camacho, p. vii.

17 David C. Culver and Tanja Pipan, *The Biology of Caves and Other Subterranean Habitats* (Oxford, 2009), p. 40.

18 See Belles, 'From Dragons to Allozymes', p. 8.

19 Culver and Pipan, *The Biology of Caves*, p. 67.

20 Tanja Pipan and David C. Culver, 'Convergence and Divergence in the Subterranean Realm: A Reassessment', *Biological Journal of the Linnean Society*, CVII (2012), p. 1.

21 Christopher Merrill, *Only the Nails Remain: Scenes from the Balkan Wars* (Lanham, MA, 2001), p. 100.

22 Quoted ibid., p. 100.

23 David Gillieson, *Caves: Processes, Development, Management* (Oxford, 1996), p. 213; Pipan and Culver, 'Convergence and Divergence', p. 1. The term 'stygobite' is of such recent coinage that it does not appear in the *Oxford English Dictionary*. It shares the etymology of the adjectives 'stygian' and 'stygial', both of which relate to the mythological river Styx, over which the spirits of the dead were ferried to Hades.

24 Jim Morrison, *The Lords and the New Creatures* (New York, 1971), p. 20.

25 Sylvia Plath, 'Nick and the Candlestick', in *Collected Poems* (New York, 2008), p. 240.

26 Kenneth Slessor, 'Sleep', in *The Penguin Book of Modern Australian Poetry*, ed. John Tranter and Philip Mead (Ringwood, VIC, 1991), pp. 9–10.

27 Bjerck, 'On the Outer Fringe of the Human World', p. 48.

28 J.R.R. Tolkien, *The Fellowship of the Ring*, 2nd edn (London, 1966), p. 63.

29 J.R.R. Tolkien, *The Hobbit* [1937] (London, 1996), p. 67.

30 Tolkien, *The Fellowship of the Ring*, p. 63.

31 Tolkien, *The Hobbit*, p. 67.

32 Ibid.

33 Pere Alberch, 'Foreword', in *The Natural History of Biospeleology*, ed. Camacho, p. v.

34 Culver and Pipan, *The Biology of Caves*, p. 1.

35 Moseley, 'Size Matters', p. 89.

36 Ibid.

37 Ibid.

38 Max Moseley, 'Are All Caves Ecotones?' *Cave and Karst Science*, XXXVI/2 (2009), p. 56.

39 See Aldemaro Romero, 'Biospeleologists', in *Encyclopedia of Caves and Karst Science*, ed. John Gunn (New York, 2004), p. 152; Trevor Shaw, *History of Cave Science: The Exploration and Study of Limestone Caves, to 1900*, 2nd edn (Sydney, 1992), p. 228; and Boris Sket, 'Can We Agree on an Ecological Classification of Subterranean Animals?', *Journal of Natural History*, LXII/21–2 (2008), p. 1550.

40 Sket, 'Can We Agree', p. 1550.

41 Mick Day and Bill Mueller, 'Aves (Birds)', in *Encyclopedia of Caves and Karst Science*, ed. Gunn, p. 130.

42 Sket, 'Can We Agree', p. 1550.

43 Gillieson, *Caves*, p. 205.

44 Culver and Pipan, *The Biology of Caves*, pp. 155–6.

45 *Planet Earth*, BBC, 2006.

46 See Cave Dweller Videos, Caves and Facts; www.bbc.co.uk/nature, accessed 30 May 2013.

47 Bjerck, 'On the Outer Fringe of the Human World', p. 59.

48 Elke Aden, 'Adaptation to Darkness', in *Encyclopedia of Caves*, ed. David C. Culver and William B. White (Burlington, MA, 2005), p. 1.

49 Ibid., p. 1.

50 Sket, 'Can We Agree', p. 1553.

51 Culver and White, *Encyclopedia of Caves*, p. 629.

52 Pipan and Culver, 'Convergence and Divergence', p. 1.

53 Ibid., p. 2.

54 Ibid., p. 8.

55 The term 'allobiosphere' was coined by G. Evelyn Hutchinson in his book *The Ecological Theater and the Evolutionary Play* (New Haven, CT, 1965). See John S. Edwards, 'Life in the Allobiosphere', *Trends in Ecology and Evolution*, III/5 (1998), p. 111.

56 Jan F. Simek, 'Archaeology of Caves: History', in *Encyclopedia of Caves and Karst Science*, ed. Gunn, p. 80.

4 Cavers, Potholers and Spelunkers: Exploring Caves

1 C.H.D. Cullingford, ed., *British Caving: An Introduction to*

Speleology (London, 1953), p. 3.

2 Trevor Shaw, *History of Cave Science: The Exploration and Study of Limestone Caves, to 1900*, 2nd edn (Sydney, 1992), p. 5.

3 Edmund J. Mason, *Caves and Caving in Britain* (London, 1977), p. 11.

4 W. Boyd Dawkins, *Cave Hunting: Researches on the Evidence of Caves Respecting the Early Inhabitants of Europe* (London, 1874), p. 22; Cary J. Griffiths, *Opening Goliath: Danger and Discovery in Caving* (St Pauls, MN, 2009), p. x.

5 Norbert Casteret, 'Discovering the Oldest Statues in the World', *National Geographic Magazine*, XLVI/2 (1924), p. 143.

6 George Crothers, P. Willey and Patty Jo Watson, 'Cave Archaeology and the NSS; 1941–2006', *Journal of Cave and Karst Studies*, LXIX/1 (2007), p. 28.

7 Ibid., p. 30.

8 Logan McNatt, 'Cave Archaeology of Belize', *Journal of Cave and Karst Studies*, LVIII/2 (1996), p. 83.

9 Dimitrij Mlekuž, 'Notes from the Underground: Caves and People in the Mesolithic and Neolithic Karst', in *Caves in Context: The Cultural Significance of Caves and Rockshelters in Europe* (Oxford, 2012), p. 203.

10 Eamon Grennan, *Out of Sight: New and Selected Poems* (Minneapolis, MN, 2010), p. 61.

11 Howard M. Beck, *Gaping Gill: 150 Years of Exploration* (London, 1984), pp. 24–7.

12 Mason, *Caves and Caving in Britain*, p. 112.

13 Edward Calvert, 'Gaping Ghyll Hole', *Yorkshire Ramblers' Club Journal*, I/1 (1889), p. 68.

14 Beck, *Gaping Gill*, p. 32.

15 Mason, *Caves and Caving in Britain*, pp. 112, 128, 168.

16 E. A. Martel, 'The Descent of Gaping Ghyll (Yorkshire), A Story of Mountaineering Reversed', *Alpine Journal*, XVIII/132 (1896), p. 121.

17 Andy Sparrow, *The Complete Caving Manual*, revd edn (Ramsbury, 2009), p. 143.

18 Mason, *Caves and Caving in Britain*, p. 42.

19 Ernest E. Roberts, 'Edouard Alfred Martel (1859–1938)', *Yorkshire Ramblers' Club Journal*, VII/24 (1947), p. 112.

20 Norbert Casteret, *Ten Years Under the Earth*, trans. Barrows Mussey (London, 1939, 1963), p. xii.

21 Ibid., p. 124.

22 Norbert Casteret, *The Darkness under the Earth* (London, 1954), p. 157.

23 Pierre Chevalier, *Subterranean Climbers: Twelve Years in the World's*

Deepest Chasm, trans. E. M. Hatt (London, 1951), p. 119.

24 Christophe Gauchon, 'France: History', in *Encyclopedia of Caves and Karst Science*, ed. John Gunn (New York, 2004), p. 371.

25 Robert K. Murray and Roger W. Brucker, *Trapped!: The Story of the Struggle to Rescue Floyd Collins from a Kentucky Cave in 1925, an Ordeal that Became One of the Most Sensational News Events of Modern Times* (New York, 1979), pp. 41–2.

26 Ibid., p. 58.

27 Patricia Kambesis, 'The Importance of Cave Exploration to Scientific Research', *Journal of Cave and Karst Studies*, LXIX/1 (2007), p. 46.

28 David W. Hughes, *Vertical Bill: The Story of Bill Cuddington and the Development of Vertical Caving in America* (Huntsville, AL, 2008), p. 315.

29 Roger W. Bruckner and Richard A. Watson, *The Longest Cave* (New York, 1976), p. 192.

30 William B. White, 'A Brief History of Karst Hydrogeology: Contributions of the NSS', *Journal of Cave and Karst Studies*, LXIX/1 (2007), p. 15.

31 Michael Ray Taylor, *Cave Passages: Roaming the Underground Wilderness* (New York, 1996), p. 56.

32 Ibid.

33 Ibid.

34 Ibid., p. 58.

35 James M. Tabor, *Blind Descent: The Quest to Discover the Deepest Cave on Earth* (London, 2011), p. ix.

36 Ibid., cover blurb.

37 Interview with James M. Tabor, *All Things Considered*, NPR, 15 July 2011. Available online at www.npr.org.

38 Tabor, *Blind Descent*, pp. x–xi.

39 'Do Cavers Prefer Doing It with the Lights Out?', interview with Jason Gardner, *Breakfast with Ryk Goddard*, 936 ABC Hobart, 14 May 2013. Available online at http://blogs.abc.net.au.

40 Norbert Casteret, 'Discovering the Oldest Statues in the World', *The National Geographic Magazine*, XLVI/2 (1924), p. 131.

41 Ibid., p. 135.

42 Eric Brymer, Greg Downey and Tonia Gray, 'Extreme Sports as a Precursor to Environmental Sustainability', *Journal of Sport and Tourism*, XIV/2–3 (2009), p. 194.

43 Quoted in Phillip Finch, *Raising the Dead* (London, 2008), p. 296.

44 Ibid., p. 239.

45 Andrew Todhunter, 'Bahamas Caves: Deep Dark Secrets', National Geographic Magazine, August 2010, http://ngm.nationalgeographic.com.

46 Interview with sbs Radio in Polish. English transcript available online at www.agnesmilowka.com.

47 Sheck Exley, *Caverns Measureless to Man* (St Louis, MO, 1994), p. 7.

48 Martyn Farr, *The Darkness Beckons: The History and Development of Cave Diving* (London, 1991), p. 7.

49 Exley, *Caverns Measureless to Man*, pp. 6-7.

50 Bill Stone, 'Foreword', in Farr, *The Darkness Beckons*, p. 12.

5 Monsters and Magic: Caves in Mythology and Folklore

1 Michael Ray Taylor, *Cave Passages: Roaming the Underground Wilderness* (New York, 1996), pp. 192–3.

2 Aeschylus, *Prometheus Bound and Other Plays*, trans. Philip Vellacott (London, 1961), p. 31.

3 Virgil, *Aeneid*, trans. Frederick Ahl (Oxford, 2007), pp. 190–91.

4 Thomas Hobbes, 'De Mirabilibus Pecci: Being the Wonders of the Peaks in Darbyshire, commonly called The Devil's Arse of Peak', trans. a Person of Quality (London, 1678), pp. 74–80.

5 Homer, *The Odyssey*, trans. Robert Fagles (New York, 1996), p. 218.

6 Ibid., p. 274.

7 Ibid., p. 212.

8 Chris Tolan-Smith, 'Folklore and Mythology' in *Encyclopedia of Caves and Karst Science*, ed. John Gunn (New York, 2004), p. 364.

9 Mary Shelley, *The Last Man*, ed. Anne McWhir (Peterborough, ONT, 1996), pp. 1–2.

10 Geoffrey Hill, *Selected Poems* (London, 2006), p. 17.

11 Cited in Trevor Shaw, *History of Cave Science: The Exploration and Study of Limestone Caves, to 1900*, 2nd edn (Sydney, 1992), p. 176.

12 Pausanias, *Description of Greece*, trans. W.H.S. Jones (London, 1918), 10.32.7. Available online at www.theoi.com.

13 See 'Dunmore', www.visitunderground.com, accessed 17 August 2011.

14 A. W. Moore, *The Folklore of the Isle of Man* (Douglas, IOM, 1891), p. 55.

15 Tony Oldham and Keith Jones, *The Caves of the South Eastern Outcrop* (Crymych, Dyfed, 1991), n.p.

16 See Harold Courlander, *The Fourth World of the Hopis: The Epic Story of the Hopi Indians as Preserved in Their Legends and Traditions* (New York, 1971), pp. 17–33.

17 Nicholas J. Saunders, 'At the Mouth of the Obsidian Cave: Deity and Place in Aztec Religion', in *Sacred Sites, Sacred Places*, ed. David L. Carmichael, et al. (London, 1994), p. 176.

18 Allen Ginsberg, 'Siesta in Xbalba,' in *Reality Sandwiches* (San Francisco, CA, 1963), p. 27.

19 See Margaret Orbell, *The Illustrated Encyclopedia of Maori Myth and Legend* (Christchurch, NZ, 1995).

20 Ian D. Clark, 'The Abode of Malevolent Spirits and Creatures – Caves in Victorian Aboriginal Social Organization', *Helictite*, XL/1 (2007), p. 10.

21 Josephine Flood, *Rock Art of the Dreamtime: Images of Ancient Australia* (Sydney, 1997), p. 27.

6 Visually Rendered: The Art of Caves

1 Paul G. Bahn, *Cave Art: A Guide to the Decorated Ice Age Caves of Europe* (London, 2012), p. 157.

2 John Canady, *What is Art? An Introduction to Painting, Sculpture and Architecture* (London, 1980), pp. 228–9.

3 Christine Niven et al, *Lonely Planet India*, 8th edn (Melbourne, 1999), p. 824.

4 Andrea Stone, 'Art: Cave Art in the Americas', in *Encyclopedia of Caves and Karst Science*, ed. John Gunn (New York, 2004), p. 92.

5 Charles H. Faulkner, 'Four Thousand Years of Native American Cave Art in the Southern Appalachians', *Journal of Cave and Karst Studies*, LIX/3 (1997), pp. 148, 152.

6 Stone, 'Art: Cave Art in the Americas', p. 91.

7 Robert G. Bednarik, 'The Cave Petroglyphs of Australia', *Australian Aboriginal Studies*, 2 (1990), pp. 64–8.

8 Paul G. Bahn and Jean Vertut, *Journey Through the Ice Age*, 2nd edn (Berkeley and Los Angeles, CA, 1997), p. 33; Josephine Flood, *Rock Art of the Dreamtime: Images of Ancient Australia* (Sydney, 1997), p. 25.

9 See Robert Bednarik, 'Art: Cave Art in Australasia', in *Encyclopedia of Caves and Karst Science*, ed. John Gunn (New York, 2004), pp. 88–90, and Bahn and Vertut, *Journey Through the Ice Age*, pp. 33–41.

10 Bahn and Vertut, *Journey Through the Ice Age*, p. 39.

11 Flood, *Rock Art of the Dreamtime*, p. 91.

12 Stephen Harris, Don Ranson and Steve Brown, 'Maxwell River Archaeological Survey 1986', *Australian Archaeology*, 27 (1988), p. 94.

13 Flood, *Rock Art of the Dreamtime*, p. 226.

14 'Historical Affairs', *Scots Magazine*, XXXIV (November 1772), p. 637.

15 John Keats, *Selected Letters*, ed. Robert Gittings (Oxford, 2002), p. 133.

16 Gerald Finley, *Landscapes of Memory: Turner as Illustrator to Scott* (Berkeley and Los Angeles, CA, 1980), pp. 138–40.

17 Michael Shortland, 'Darkness Visible: Underground Culture in the Golden Age of Geology', *History of Science*, XXXII (1994), p. 10.
18 Cosmo Landesman, 'Genius with a Spray Can, but is it Art?', *Sunday Times* (20 July 2003).
19 Chris Howes, *To Photograph Darkness: The History of Underground and Flash Photography* (Gloucester, 1989), p. 34.
20 Maria Walsh, *Art and Psychoanalysis* (New York, 2013), p. 18.

7 'Caverns measureless to man': Caves in Literature

1 Samuel Taylor Coleridge, 'Kubla Khan', in *The Major Works*, ed. H. J. Jackson (Oxford, 2008), p. 103.
2 Ibid.
3 Ibid., pp. 103–4.
4 W. H. Auden, 'In Praise of Limestone', in *Collected Poems*, ed. Edward Mendelson (New York, 1991), p. 540.
5 Robert Macfarlane, *The Wild Places* [2007] (London, 2008), pp. 173–4.
6 Robert Penn Warren, 'Speleology', in *The Collected Poems of Robert Penn Warren*, ed. John Burt (Baton Rouge, LA, 1998), p. 382.
7 Gaston Bachelard, *La terre et les rêveries du repos* [1948] (Paris, 1971), p. 193.
8 Warren, 'Speleology', p. 382.
9 William Shakespeare, *Henry V* (11.iv.129).
10 Wilfred Stone, *The Cave and the Mountain* (Stanford, CA, 1966), p. 307.
11 Daniel Defoe, *Robinson Crusoe*, ed. J. Donald Crowley (Oxford, 1983), p. 179.
12 Ibid., p. 69.
13 Ibid., p. 177.
14 Ibid., pp. 178–9.
15 Michel Tournier, *Friday*, trans. Norman Denny (Baltimore, MD, 1997), p. 101.
16 E. A. Martel, 'Speleology, or Cave Exploration', *Appleton's Popular Science Monthly*, LIV (1899), p. 257.
17 J.R.R. Tolkien, *The Two Towers*, 2nd edn (London, 1966), p. 152.
18 Michael Drayton, 'An Ode Written in the Peake', in *The Works of Michael Drayton*, ed. J. William Hebel, vol. II (Oxford, 1932), p. 365.
19 William Camden, *Britannia*, trans. Philomen Holland (London, 1610), p. 557; Ben Jonson, *The Gypsies Metamorphosed*, in *Ben Jonson*, ed. C. H. Hereford and Percy and Evelyn Simpson (Oxford, 1941), vol. VII, p. 569.
20 Bachelard, *La terre et les rêveries du repos*, p. 10.

21 Jules Verne, *Journey to the Centre of the Earth*, trans. William Butcher (Oxford, 2008), p. 118.
22 Ibid., p. 139.
23 Mark Twain, *The Adventures of Tom Sawyer*, ed. Peter Stoneley (Oxford, 2008), p. 162.
24 See Verne, *Journey to the Centre of the Earth*, pp. 225–6.
25 Twain, *Tom Sawyer*, p. 162.
26 Richard Church, *The Cave* (London, 1983), p. 16.
27 Stephen Crane, 'Four Men in a Cave', in *Sullivan County Tales and Sketches*, ed. R. W. Stallman (Ames, IA, 1968), p. 72.
28 Ibid., p. 73.
29 'Evelyn Waugh', *Life* (8 April 1946), p. 53.

8 Sacred Symbols: Holy Caves

1 Genesis 23:19; 25:9.
2 See Genesis 49:31 and 50:13.
3 Amitav Ghosh, *River of Smoke* (London, 2011), pp. 7–8.
4 George Crothers, P. Willey and Patty Jo Watson, 'Cave Archaeology and the NSS: 1941–2006', *Journal of Cave and Karst Studies*, LXIX/1 (2007), p. 28.
5 G. E. Robson, 'The Caves of Sof Omar', *Geographical Journal*, CXXXIII/3 (1967), p. 345.
6 Ibid., p. 346.
7 D. Caitlin, 'The Caves of Ethiopia', *Transactions of the Cave Research Group of Great Britain*, XV/3 (1973), pp. 107–68.
8 Vicki Mackenzie, *Caves in the Snow: Tenzin Palmo's Quest for Enlightenment* (London, 1998), p. 198.
9 'Equipment Light System Installation in Slovenia', www.cavelighting.com, accessed 30 May 2013.
10 Georg Gerster, *Churches in Rock: Early Christian Art in Ethiopia*, trans. Richard Hosking (London, 1970), p. 110.
11 V. C. Scott O'Connor, *The Silken East: A Record of Life and Travel in Burma* (London, 1904), vol. II, pp. 614–17.

9 Extraordinary to Behold: Spectacular Caves

1 Andy Sparrow, *The Complete Caving Manual*, revd edn (Ramsbury, 2009), p. 9.
2 Norbert Casteret, *Ten Years Under the Earth*, trans. Barrows Mussey (London, 1963), p. xii.
3 Arrigo A. Cigna, 'Show Caves', in *Encyclopedia of Caves*, ed. David C. Culver and William B. White (Burlington, MA, 2005), pp. 495–6.

4 D. J. Irwin, 'Gough's Old Cave: Its History', *Proceedings University of Bristol Spelaeological Society*, XVII/3 (1986), p. 262.

5 T. R. Shaw, 'Martel's Visit to Mendip in 1904: Part of his International Strategy?', *Proceedings of the University of Bristol Spelaeological Society*, XVII/3 (1986), p. 281.

6 Charles W. Wright, *A Guide Manual to the Mammoth Cave of Kentucky* (Louisville, KY, 1860), p. 9.

7 Anthony Trollope, *Australia and New Zealand* [1873] (London, 1968), vol. II, p. 45.

8 Elery Hamilton-Smith, 'Tourism and Caves: History', in *Encyclopedia of Caves and Karst Science*, ed. John Gunn (New York, 2004), p. 726.

9 Russell Gurnee and Jeanne Gurnee, *Gurnee Guide to American Caves* (Closter, NJ, 1990), p. 122.

10 Randy Tufts and Gary Tenen, 'Discovery and History of Kartchner Caverns, Arizona', *Journal of Cave and Karst Studies*, LXI/2 (1999), p. 44.

11 'Park Rules: Cave Tours', http://azstateparks.com, accessed 15 November 2011.

12 Barbara Hurd, *Entering the Stone: On Caves and Feeling through the Dark* (Athens, GA, 2008), p. 50.

13 Ibid., pp. 49–61.

14 Kath Walker, 'Returned Pearl Cave', in *Kath Walker in China* (Brisbane, 1988), p. 49.

15 Kath Walker, 'Reed Flute Cave', in *Kath Walker in China* (Brisbane, 1998), p. 53.

16 See R.A.L. Osborne, H. Zwingermann, R. E. Pogson and D. M. Colchester, 'Carboniferous Clay Deposits from Jenolan Caves, New South Wales: Implications for Timing of Speleogenesis and Regional Geology', *Australian Journal of Earth Sciences*, LIII/3 (2006), pp. 377–405.

17 Elery Hamilton-Smith, 'Tourist Caves', in *Encylopedia of Caves and Karst Science*, ed. John Gunn (New York, 2004), p. 727.

18 See www.waitomo.co.nz/HaggasHonkingHoles, accessed 24 August 2011.

SELECT BIBLIOGRAPHY

Bahn, Paul G., *Cave Art: A Guide to the Decorated Ice Age Caves of Europe* (London, 2012)

Bergsvik, Knut Andreas, and Robin Skeates, eds, *Caves in Context: The Cultural Significance of Caves and Rockshelters in Europe* (Oxford, 2012)

Bruckner, Roger W., and Richard A. Watson, *The Longest Cave* (New York, 1976)

Casteret, Norbert, *Ten Years Under the Earth*, trans. Barrows Mussey (London, 1939)

Chevalier, Pierre, *Subterranean Climbers: Twelve Years in the World's Deepest Chasm*, trans. E. M. Hatt (London, 1951)

Cullingford, C.H.D., ed., *British Caving: An Introduction to Speleology* (London, 1953)

Culver, David C., and Tanja Pipan, *The Biology of Caves and Other Subterranean Habitats* (Oxford, 2009)

Culver, David C., and William B. White, eds, *Encyclopedia of Caves* (Burlington, MA, 2005)

Exley, Sheck, *Caverns Measureless to Man* (St Louis, MO, 1994)

Eyre, Jim, and John Frankland, *Race Against Time: A History of the Cave Rescue Organisation* (Sedbergh, 1988)

Farr, Martyn, *The Darkness Beckons: The History and Development of Cave Diving* (London, 1991)

Finlayson, Brian, and Elery Hamilton-Smith, eds, *Beneath the Surface: A Natural History of Australian Caves* (Sydney, 2003)

Gillieson, David, *Caves: Processes, Development, Management* (Oxford, 1996)

Gunn, John, ed., *Encyclopedia of Caves and Karst Science* (New York, 2004)

Heinerth, Jill, *The Essentials of Cave Diving* (High Springs, FL, 2010)

Howes, Chris, *To Photograph Darkness: The History of Underground and Flash Photography* (Gloucester, 1989)

Hurd, Barbara, *Entering the Stone: On Caves and Feeling through the Dark* (Athens, GA, 2008)

Joly, Robert de, *Memoirs of a Speleologist: The Adventurous Life of a Famous French Explorer*, trans. Peter Kurz (Teaneck, NJ, 1975)

Palmer, Arthur N., *Cave Geology* (Dayton, OH, 2007)

Shaw, Trevor R., *History of Cave Science: The Exploration and Study of Limestone Caves, to 1900*, 2nd edn (Sydney, 1992)

Sparrow, Andy, *The Complete Caving Manual*, revd edn (Ramsbury, 2009)

Tabor, James M., *Blind Descent: The Quest to Discover the Deepest Place on Earth* (New York, 2010)

Taylor, Michael Ray, *Cave Passages: Roaming the Underground Wilderness* (New York, 1996)

ASSOCIATIONS AND WEBSITES

Association of British and Irish Show Caves
www.visitunderground.com
Association for the protection and conservation of underground
tourism sites across Britain and Ireland

Australasian Cave and Karst Management Association
www.ackma.org
Professional association dedicated to the management of
Australasian caves and karst landscapes. The site includes articles
for the association's journal and information about conferences and
research opportunities

Australian Speleological Federation
www.caves.org.au
An environmental organization whose primary objective is karst
conservation. It represents Australia on the International Union of
Speleology, and the interests of 28 caving clubs

British Cave Rescue Council
www.caverescue.org.uk
The representative body for voluntary underground rescue in the
British Isles. It is part of the European Cave Rescue Network

British Cave Research Association
www.bcra.org.uk
Research arm of the British Caving Association

British Caving Association
www.british-caving.org.uk
The governing body for underground exploration in the UK

International Show Caves Association
   www.i-s-c-a.com
   A site with multiple resources for learning about show caves

International Union of Speleology
   www.uis-speleo.org
   The international body for caving and speleology

National Speleological Society (USA)
   www.caves.org
   National body for the study, exploration and conservation of cave
   and karst environments in the United States. Includes a link to the
   online *Journal of Cave and Karst Studies*

Show Caves
   www.showcaves.com
   A comprehensive index to caves, karst, springs, mines and
   subterranea around the world, maintained by Jochen Duckeck

Speleobooks
   www.speleobooks.com
   The world's leading online bookshop for cave enthusiasts

Speleogenesis
   www.speleogenesis.info
   A scientific network promoting research in karst hydrogeology.
   It includes a link to KarstBase, which offers a searchable online
   database of current karst research

ACKNOWLEDGEMENTS

The research and writing of this book was expedited by several grants and periods of study leave. We would like to thank the University of Tasmania for granting us each a period of study leave during which the bulk of the research and writing was carried out, and for funding various research trips to caves, conferences and archives. We would also like to express our gratitude to the Arts and Environment Research Group in the Faculty of Arts, which provided financial assistance towards the cost of permission fees to reproduce the illustrations.

Our colleagues in the UTAS English programme were a patient audience for our adventures in speleology; in particular, we are indebted to Elizabeth Leane for the feedback she provided on our chapter drafts. We appreciate the assistance provided by Rachel Adams in the Document Delivery section of the Morris Miller Library, who tracked down illustrations from rare books.

We would like to thank Elery Hamilton-Smith for generously sharing his knowledge of caves with us; Deb Hunter for caving trips; the Bradford Pothole Club for Ralph Crane's descent into Gaping Ghyll; Richard Williams for photographing our caves memorabilia; and Stephen Fletcher for his drawing of a cross-section of a cave.

Members of our families have lived through the writing of this book with exemplary patience and surprising enthusiasm, and they have happily followed us underground on several occasions.

Finally, our thanks go to Michael Leaman and Daniel Allen for giving us the opportunity to embark on this adventure, and the team at Reaktion Books for guiding the book to publication.

Permission
Judith Beveridge, 'How to Love Bats', on pp. 42–3 © *Accidental Grace* by Judith Beveridge, University of Queensland Press, 1996.

PHOTO ACKNOWLEDGEMENTS

The author and publishers wish to express their thanks to the below sources of illustrative material and/or permission to reproduce it. The authors have made every effort to trace the original copyright holders and would welcome correspondence via the publishers from those they have been unable to trace.

From W. H. Davenport Adams, *Famous Caverns and Grottoes Described and Illustrated* (London, 1886): p. 17; map art by Jackie Aher: p. 141; courtesy of The Approach London (image credit Alex Delfanne): p. 123; from *Archæological and Historical Collections relating to Ayrshire and Galloway*, Vol. v. (Edinburgh, 1885): p. 150; image © Art Resource, NY: p. 15; collection of the authors: pp. 35, 50, 80, 82, 94, 106, 160, 163, 164–5, 168, 179, 184; photo by Martin Baines: p. 128; photos by Steve Bourne: pp. 32, 36, 44, 55, 59, 60, 64, 112, 172; image © The British Library Board (012633.g.16): p. 137; image © The British Library Board (12516.f.33): p. 140; image © Trustees of the British Museum, London: p. 133; from Richard Church, *The Cave* (Harmondsworth, 1950 – cover reproduced with permission of Penguin Books Ltd): p. 142; from Samuel Taylor Coleridge, *Kubla Khan* (Reading, 2004) – reproduced with permission from Two Rivers Press (© images and lettering Peter Hay and Pip Hall, 2004): p. 126; photo Joy Crane: p. 71; photos by Ralph Crane: pp. 11, 23, 24–5, 30, 39, 57, 62, 68, 75, 85, 100–101, 158, 167, 173, 174–5, 176, 178, 180–81; from C.H.D. Cullingford, *British Caving: An Introduction to Speleology* (London, 1953): p. 67; from Gustave Doré, *La Sainte Bible* (Tours, 1866): p. 146; illustration by Stephen Fletcher: p. 10; photo courtesy of Jill Heinerth: p. 88; photo by Michael Leaman/Reaktion Books: p. 152; image © The Metropolitan Museum of Art/image source Art Resource, NY: pp. 15, 121; from Jeff Parker and Steve Lieber, *Underground* (Berkeley, CA, 2010), reproduced courtesy of ImageComics: p. 14; private collection/The Bridgeman Art Library: p. 119; from Robert Sanders, *The Complete English Traveller: or, a New Survey and Description*

INDEX